NEW ESSAYS ON INVISIBLE MAN

★ The American Novel ★

GENERAL EDITOR

Emory Elliott, Princeton University

New Essays on Invisible Man

Edited by

Robert O'Meally

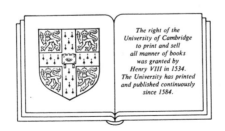

The right of the
University of Cambridge
to print and sell
all manner of books
was granted by
Henry VIII in 1534.
The University has printed
and published continuously
since 1584.

CAMBRIDGE UNIVERSITY PRESS

Cambridge

New York   New Rochelle   Melbourne   Sydney

Published by the Press Syndicate of the University of Cambridge
The Pitt Building, Trumpington Street, Cambridge CB2 1RP
32 East 57th Street, New York, NY 10022, USA
10 Stamford Road, Oakleigh, Melbourne 3166, Australia

First published 1988

Printed in the United States of America

Library of Congress Cataloging-in-Publication Data
New essays on Invisible man.
(The American novel)
Bibliography: p.
1. Ellison, Ralph. Invisible man. I. O'Meally,
Robert G., 1948–   . II. Series.
PS3555.L625I536   1988   813'.54   87-22415

ISBN 0 521 30896 8 hard covers
ISBN 0 521 31369 4 paperback

British Library Cataloguing in Publication data applied for.

Contents

v

Contents

Series Editor's Preface

In literary criticism the last twenty-five years have been particularly fruitful. Since the rise of the New Criticism in the 1950s, which focused attention of critics and readers upon the text itself – apart from history, biography, and society – there has emerged a wide variety of critical methods which have brought to literary works a rich diversity of perspectives: social, historical, political, psychological, economic, ideological, and philosophical. While attention to the text itself, as taught by the New Critics, remains at the core of contemporary interpretation, the widely shared assumption that works of art generate many different kinds of interpretation has opened up possibilities for new readings and new meanings.

Before this critical revolution, many American novels had come to be taken for granted by earlier generations of readers as having an established set of recognized interpretations. There was a sense among many students that the canon was established and that the larger thematic and interpretative issues had been decided. The task of the new reader was to examine the ways in which elements such as structure, style, and imagery contributed to each novel's acknowledged purpose. But recent criticism has brought these old assumptions into question and has thereby generated a wide variety of original, and often quite surprising, interpretations of the classics, as well as of rediscovered novels such as Kate Chopin's *The Awakening*, which has only recently entered the canon of works that scholars and critics study and that teachers assign their students.

The aim of The American Novel Series is to provide students of American literature and culture with introductory critical guides to

American novels now widely read and studied. Each volume is devoted to a single novel and begins with an introduction by the volume editor, a distinguished authority on the text. The introduction presents details of the novel's composition, publication history, and contemporary reception, as well as a survey of the major critical trends and readings from first publication to the present. This overview is followed by four or five original essays, specifically commissioned from senior scholars of established reputation and from outstanding younger critics. Each essay presents a distinct point of view, and together they constitute a forum of interpretative methods and of the best contemporary ideas on each text.

It is our hope that these volumes will convey the vitality of current critical work in American literature, generate new insights and excitement for students of the American novel, and inspire new respect for and new perspectives upon these major literary texts.

Emory Elliott
Princeton University

1

Introduction

ROBERT O'MEALLY

. . . You just write for your own time, while trying to write in terms of
the density of experience, knowing perfectly well that life repeats
itself. Even in this rapidly changing United States it repeats itself. The
mystery is that while repeating itself it always manages slightly to
change its mask. To be able to grasp a little of that change within
continuity, to communicate it across all these divisions of background and individual experience, seems enough for me. If you're
lucky, of course, if you splice into one of the deeper currents of life,
then you have a chance of your work lasting a little longer.[1]
                                                          −Ralph Ellison

. . . The racial turmoil as we know it . . . was only a distant thunder,
not necessarily promising rain. In that state of nervous calm, Ellison
could produce a novel which, regarding the character and fate of
American Negroes − indeed the character and fate of our whole
multi-racial society − was both a summation and a prophesy.[2]
                                                          −F. W. Dupee

PUBLISHED a mere thirty-five years ago, Ralph Ellison's *Invisible Man* shares with older classic works the odd quality of
seeming to have been in place for much longer, if not forever. It is
a novel that encompasses much of the American scene and character; though told by a single Afro-American and set in the contemporary South and then in modern New York City, its references are to the First World War, to Reconstruction, to the Civil
War and slavery, to the founding of the republic, to Columbus,
and to the country's frontier past. *Invisible Man* delves deeply into
what R. W. B. Lewis, an early commentator on the novel, has
termed "our representative native theme": "For if there is an
American fiction it is this − " wrote Lewis in 1953, "the adventures likely to befall a centerless individual en route through the
flow and conflict of illusions toward some still undisclosed cen-

1

ter."[3] (Lewis's phrasing brings to mind the convincing argument, on the part of Ellison critics, that this novel of the "adventures" of a "centerless individual" is a book of the blues.)[4] Not only does this novel summarize, in artistic terms, so much Americana, but its allusions to world literature and its structural underpinnings in myth and ritual, transcending particular place and time, grant the work resounding depth and scope. Some recent critics have even seen in *Invisible Man* a strange *precognitive* power:[5] Its young hero's mix of idealism and alienation, his escapes into music, marijuana, and gadgetry; the book's study of interracial angst and urban riot; its exploration of the relation of the "Woman Question" to the Afro-American freedom struggle; its dangerous, false-faced establishmentarians in politics, education, and business; and its equally lethal "saviors" like Ras and Rinehart — all seem to belong to an era *after* the one in which the novel first appeared.

Invisible Man recalls, and often makes specific reference to, the beginnings of the novel as a literary form: to Cervantes, Fielding, Defoe and, more significantly, to works by great nineteenth-century novelists, Twain, James, Dostoievsky, and especially Melville,[6] who provides one of the book's epigraphs. Like *Moby Dick, Invisible Man* is a capacious novel, one that tries many things: Both are rhetorical tours de force containing letters, sermons, fights, songs, political speeches, dreams, and descriptions of private homes, meeting halls, offices, brothels, bars, and churches. Ellison's is a realistic novel evoking particular places in exact detail; but it is also a surrealistic work, challenging its reader to fit together its baffling dream pieces. As tradition-conscious and summarizing as this novel is, it manages, through eloquent, experimental play with form and idiom, to seem even younger than its years. And like *bovaryism, invisibility* is a metaphor that has moved from its original literary context to become a key metaphor for its era.

As one critic has pointed out, *Invisible Man* is probably the finest first novel since Thomas Mann's *Buddenbrooks;* it is much more mature than the first novels of Faulkner, Hemingway, and Fitzgerald,[7] and indeed compares with their best work. How did this first novel by an unknown writer come to be known as a classic in so short a time? To demystify this classic-making process somewhat, we should observe that its publisher, Random House, marketed it as a special achievement right from the beginning.[8] The book's first edition, issued in the spring of 1952, proclaimed it "a monumental novel, one that can well be called an epic of modern American Negro life." Advance copies were sent to reviewers considered able to deal with such a complexly challenging work, with such a *novel* novel. Journals shaping any book's initial public reception — *The New York Times, The New Republic, The New Yorker, Time, The Saturday Review* — all reviewed the book prominently (*The Times* reviewed it twice) and with unanimous, if not unqualified, favor. Many reviewers considered the book somewhat overwrought and prolix, but virtually all recognized its importance as literature. When the novel was first published, Wright Morris announced grandly that it "belongs on the shelf with classical efforts to chart the river Lethe from its mouth to its source."[9] Influential quarterlies assigned the book to such prestigious scholar/writers as Richard Chase, R. W. B. Lewis, and Delmore Schwartz, who were, if anything, even more enthusiastic than the newspaper reviewers. Schwartz apologized that "the language of literary criticism seems shallow and patronizing when one has to speak of a book like this . . . It is a book which ought to be reviewed by William Faulkner, the author of *Light in August*."[10] (This apt comparison of *Invisible Man* and *Light in August* is made by several of Ellison's first reviewers.)

The building of this monumental novel can be traced through its various editions. The second, third, and subsequent hardcover printings carried some of the aforementioned reviewers' heady commentary, along with glowing praise songs by Langston Hughes, Kenneth Burke, and F. W. Dupee, who called *Invisible Man* "the veritable *Moby-Dick* of the racial crisis."[11] By July 1953, Signet's fifty-cent paperback edition had made the book available "in over 100,000 bookstores, drugstores and newsstand outlets throughout the country."[12] That first paperback proudly proclaimed the novel the winner of the National Book Award and "The Blazing Best Seller of the Year." (Altogether *Invisible Man* stayed on the best-seller lists for sixteen weeks. By 1982, it had sold out twenty hardcover printings and seventeen Vintage paperback printings.) Modern Library and Penguin editions have made the book readily available throughout the English-speaking world, and it has been translated into at least fifteen languages.

Special editions further confirmed the book's staying power and coming classic status. In 1980, the Franklin Mint Library brought out a limited edition in gold and leather, illustrated, signed, and prefaced by a "special message" from Ellison tracing the magic book's genesis. Then in 1982 Random House celebrated the book's birthday with a handsome "Thirtieth Anniversary Edition" containing a still fuller introductory essay by the author. Again the work was reviewed everywhere with approval, this time with even more of the hushed awe befitting a revered text. Some reviewers who had grown up with the book said that they admired it more with each rereading and that the book's unmistakably great sections (the battle royal, the episodes involving Trueblood, Tod, and Rinehart, the riot) now totally eclipsed those fictional experiments that seemed forced or that otherwise did not work. *The Washington Post's* reviewer of 1982 was among many stating that "*Invisible Man* has as much claim to being that mythical, unattainable dream of American literature, the 'great American novel,' as any book in our literature."[13]

The National Book Award was only the most prominent prize the novel won. It also received the National Newspaper Publishers Award (1952) and *Chicago Defender's* award as the work "symbolizing the best in American democracy" (1953). In 1965, a poll by *Book Week* of two hundred prominent authors, critics, and editors judged *Invisible Man* "the most distinguished single work" published in the previous twenty years. The recipient of fifteen honorary degrees – along with the American Medal of Freedom (1969), the French Chevalier de l'Ordre des Artes et Lettres (1970), and the National Medal of Arts (1985) – Ellison has been among the most decorated of American writers.

Even more than these honors and awards, however, the academy, both in America and abroad, has given momentum to *Invisible Man's* ascent toward classic heights. By the mid-sixties, with the mounting awareness of the book as more than a best-seller, as a work of literature, along with pressure provided by the Afro-American freedom movement and by the revolution in college curricula, *Invisible Man* was quite often assigned in English and humanities courses as well as in fledgling American and Afro-American studies courses. And it has stayed on reading lists ever since, even showing up at times on creatively constructed syllabi in the social sciences. Most readers now probably first encounter the novel not through word-of-mouth recommendation (which was doubtless the case in its best-seller days), but as a homework assignment. Since 1970, master's and Ph.D. dissertations on Ellison and his novel have proliferated. Scholarly articles, anthologies of articles, a casebook of relevant readings, and since 1979, book-length studies have helped teachers and students appreciate the work. All of this academic scaffolding has been part of the classic-making process. In 1974, Jacqueline Covo's annotated bibliography, *The Blinking Eye: Ralph Waldo Ellison and his American, French, German and Italian Critics, 1952–1971,* offered comprehensive evidence that *Invisible Man* had done what its last sentence proclaims in rhetorical form: "Who knows but that, on the lower frequencies, I speak for you?"

Upon the widening shelf of Ellison criticism, one sees a bit of everything. One could fairly chart the shifting course of critical history from 1960 to 1986 by reviewing the critical approaches to this novel.[14] Ellison himself is one reader of the novel whose judgments, though by definition privileged, cannot be discounted; in fact, he has been among his own best critics. He has provided two Jamesian or Shavian[15] prefaces to his work, and he has written two superb essays, "Change the Joke and Slip the Yoke" and "The World and the Jug" (both reprinted in his first book of essays, *Shadow and Act,* 1964), specifically in response to critical pieces on his novel. And Ellison, who is interviewed quite frequently in print (two interviews appear in *Shadow and Act*), sometimes uses those occasions to counterstate a particular misconception of his novel or otherwise to offer hints as to how he wants it read. Not surprisingly, he is most irritated by those critics who overstress the book's narrowly racial or political aspects, those who prefer to see it not as a novel at all but as a sociological case study, as a document of protest, or as an untransformed report of his personal or political reminiscences. Some critics, for instance, have disliked the novel's "attack on the Communist Party"[16] (though Ellison has pointed out that the Brotherhood is neither identified in the novel as the Communist Party, nor is the party the only white-controlled American party to betray the black community). Other critics have complained blankly that not all Negroes act like the ones in this book.[17] Some have dispraised the work as an intolerably arty production, far too indirect for a time of engaged struggle; others have left-handedly praised it as the long-awaited conclusive evidence that, culturally speaking, the Negro has *arrived*. Granville Hicks, for one, says: "What such a novel as *Invisible Man* does do is to demonstrate that the American Negro is deserving of not only political and economic but cultural equality."[18]

Fortunately, from the beginning, there have been critics who have considered *Invisible Man* not as some sort of demonstration but as a work of art. There are fine studies of the novel's position within both the traditions of American vernacular literature of Twain and Hemingway and the tradition of American symbolist literature of Melville and T. S. Eliot. Several critics have discussed the novel's connections with works by Frederick Douglass and Richard Wright — and with the tradition of Afro-American narrative — as well as with works by Faulkner, Joyce, Malraux, and Dostoievsky. The novel's uses of black folklore and blues have frequently been studied; in a fine recent book, the Trueblood section of the novel is closely read in light of the economics of the blues.[19] Myth-and-archetype critics, New Critics of various kinds, critics concerned as much with historical and cultural contexts as with the naked text itself, psychological critics, structuralists, deconstructionists, and even a Marxist deconstructionist — all have contributed positively to the Ellison canon.

In the present collection, no attempt has been made to be sweepingly representative or comprehensive. The editor and other critics have, however, heeded Ellison's warning that "for the novelist, of any cultural or racial identity, his form is his greatest freedom and his insights are where he finds them."[20] Taken together, these critical pieces, all of them appearing here for the first time, pay attention to this novel as a literary form: to its strategies as an elaborated picaresque tale about a character who, as Ellison says, "possesses both the eloquence and the insight into the interconnections between his own personality and the world about him to make a judgment upon our culture."[21] Valerie Smith and Thomas Schaub examine the book's narrative strategies in light of its literary antecedents and influences, as well as its political and intellectual backgrounds. John Callahan and John Wright underscore the fact that this is a novel about a gifted public speaker, and that as such it is a meditation not just on the challenges of political leadership but on the special callings of the artist. And they are mindful of Ellison's position that "writers . . . help create or reveal hidden realities by asserting their existence";[22] thus he has spoken at times of the "sacredness" of the novelist's task.

According to Ellison, the American novel is bound up with "our problem of nationhood";[23] several of the essayists here are concerned with the Americanness of this novel and with what Callahan terms its "unabashed patriotism." Wright reminds us, too, that *Invisible Man* is a postwartime novel that meditates not just on modern wars but most specifically on America's Civil War and on certain of its unresolved dilemmas. ("I guess," Ellison observes, "that all my work is grounded in a concern with the hidden aspects of American history as they come to focus in our racial predicament.")[24] Along with other key paradigms for reading *Invisible Man*, Berndt Ostendorf considers the impact of jazz on the novel, which he sees as a masterpiece of modernism. Ellison's work, the essays and stories as well as the novel, leaves no doubt that for him jazz and other forms of music are much more than a casual influence. One is reminded of Mrs. Ellison's statement to a group of students in the 1950s that when her husband, a former music major in college and professional musician, "can't find the words at the typewriter, he goes upstairs and plays the trumpet."[25]

The pieces included here help explain the novel's fantastic appeal and what one critic termed its "strenuous circulation." F. W. Dupee wrote that *Invisible Man* is probably "one of the most thoroughly read, really *read*, novels of the time, thumbed to pieces in libraries, passed from hand to impatient hand among friends of just about every race, place and every age beyond the first stages of literacy."[26] How had Ellison found just the frequency on which to "speak for" such a widely diverse group of readers? He did so by performing the artist's primal magic of starting with an area of experience that he knew intimately – that of a talented black American youngster, deeply versed in the vernacular, who tries to take a major leadership role in a post–World War America that seems dead set against him – and by scoring that blues-toned experience in terms that were as eloquent and comprehensive as possible.

It is important to note that this did not mean writing specifically for white readers (as some black critics have charged).[27] "Too many books by Negro writers are addressed to a white audience," Ellison has said. "By doing this the authors run the risk of limiting themselves to the audience's presumptions of what a Negro is or should be; the tendency is to become involved in polemics, to plead the Negro's humanity" (*SA*,170). Rather than do this, Ellison focused his novel on issues affecting black Americans, on the lingering problem, for example, of finding black leadership that was effectively responsive to the black group's own needs and wishes. As a writer rather than a politician or social scientist, Ellison also felt called upon to celebrate those Afro-American styles and values that have sustained the group and to destroy with words those aspects of Afro-American life that have *not* been sustaining. In this sense, and in the sense that certain in-group jokes and games must be explained by black American critics to white readers, Ellison seems to have written *Invisible Man* for a *black* audience.[28] The black writers Kenneth McClane and William J. Harris both told the editor that everything that happens to them as blacks in America seems to have been covered, in one way or another, by *Invisible Man*.

Why then, some critics have asked, all the fancy quotation of white "masters" of the novel form; why all the straining after universality? Here the answer is simple: Like Duke Ellington, whose raggiest dance numbers (let us leave aside the symphonies) can contain the most complex chords, structural innovations, and interpolations from classical composers, Ellison uses everything he knows, not to prove anything to anybody but to exploit as fully as possible the artistic materials he is conjuring – to render Harlem with enough accuracy that Harlemites who read the book would recognize the place, and also to express emphatically what he once termed "the 'harlemness' of the national human predicament."[29]

Nor does this mean that Ellison's novel is exotic by design or in any way hostile to nonblacks; it merely means that as with early jazz, played at first by black musicians for black dancers and for themselves, nonblacks who wanted to get with it had to enter deeply into its rich spirit. And like good jazz, the novel beckons readers of all backgrounds. For example, even though the book's Harlem cart pusher who calls himself "Petie Wheatstraw" (having appropriated, for the moment, a black folkloric name sometimes taken by blues musicians and storytellers) speaks in thick Afro-Americanese to remind Invisible Man of his southern "colored" roots, the lingo itself is so alluringly exuberant that it is irresistible – both for Invisible Man, who at first it put off by all such talk, and for the reader. That the Petie Wheatstraw encounter is framed not just as a decorative refrain but as part of an initiation ritual – of the youngster entering the realm of grown-up complexity, of the "green" newcomer traveling from the old (down home) world to the new (urban) frontier – makes it not only a general American experience but one that is repeated worldwide. Likewise, Invisible Man's other large quests – for freedom that is neither so formless as to be chaotic (witness Rinehart) or so tightly controlled as to be mechanical or oppressive (witness Bledsoe) and, above all, for a personal identity he can live with – surely these are not only Afro-American quests. His musings in a Harlem rooming house sound like those of modern youths around the world:

> I had no doubt that I could do something, but what, and how? I had no contacts and I believed in nothing. And the obsession with my identity, which I had developed in the factory hospital had returned with a vengeance. Who was I, how had I come to be? Certainly I couldn't help being different from when I left the campus; but now a new, painful, contradictory voice had grown up within me. . . . I throbbed with guilt and puzzlement. I wanted peace and quiet, tranquility, but was too much aboil inside.[30]

The other crucial point to make here is that in his novel Ellison reaches out to the reader by raising a sheaf of intellectual issues that have disturbed and intrigued people of all backgrounds forever: What is the shape of history? What is the true relation of science, art, and politics? How does one account for human motives for action? How does one know the self? The other? By drawing such questions out of the vernacular experience of a black American character, Ellison manages to "splice into . . . the deeper currents on life," to show the universality of blackness.

That Invisible Man's memoirs are framed in a traditional form, as a novel, serves as a lure to all readers familiar with that form to enjoy its formal aspects and its "sheer narrative ride."[31] This novel's extraordinary fullness of allusions to other novels, and to other works of many kinds, literary, philosophical, psychological, political, also invites the reader deeper into the text. Poe, for example, is mentioned in *Invisible Man's* opening lines, and the novel is a kind of elaborated detective story, with the bewildered protagonist oddly cast (like Oedipus) as both detective and criminal. In time he learns that there really is a connection, as the "crazy" veteran has told him, between criminality (recall here that Tarp's crime was saying no to a white man, and Tod's was that he "thought . . . he was a man") and freedom. And as Ellison has often pointed out, a voice reminiscent of Dostoievsky's underground man's voice sounds in *Invisible Man's* Prologue, the "sick" and "guilty" words expressed this time by a brown-skinned latter-day maker of notes underground. Classical literature, fairy tales, early novels, works by major modern writers and thinkers including Freud, Marx, Eliot, Wright, Malraux, Hemingway, Faulkner — all provide allusions in *Invisible Man*. To readers who know the works alluded to, they give a cluster of reference points, familiar plots of ground to stand upon; they also send readers with initiative and curiosity to the library to look up unknown references. Indeed, this novel beckons readers not just into its own pages but into a lifetime of serious study. It is in this context, I should add, that the "obscure" references to black life and lore make all the sense in the world: Here too the point is to communicate intimately with those sharing the author's particular cultural background, and also to invite those who do not share this background to realize that black American life has its own contour and mystery and to *do some homework*.

Humor is a key — perhaps it is the master key — to the highly successful communication process of this novel. Even those who are uninitiated into Wheatstraw's word magic, or Poe's, can enjoy this book as a skillfully spun narrative and as one that is, even on

10

the surface, very, very funny. Interestingly, some of the book's earliest reviewers missed its most profound humor; for them certain humorous passages were, ironically, invisible. No doubt part of the problem here was that some jokes in the book derived from Afro-American vernacular experience, from folklore and stage shows that had not, at least by the fifties, "crossed the tracks" from black to white America. Ellison has explained, for example, that after first typing the novel's opening words, "I am an invisible man," he snatched the paper from the typewriter, intending to destroy it. Then as he began to wonder who would make such an outrageous assertion, "the words began to sound with a familiar timbre of voice":

> And suddenly I could hear in my head a blackface comedian bragging on the stage of Harlem's Apollo Theatre to the effect that each generation of his family was becoming so progressively black of complexion that no one, not even its own mother, had ever been able to see the two-year-old baby. The audience had roared with laughter, and I recognized something of the same joking, in-group Negro American irony sounding from my rumpled page.[32]

Such black in-jokes reverberate throughout this novel. For example, Lucius Brockway's inspired motto for one of Liberty Paints' products, "If It's Optic White, It's the Right White," echoes the ironic black folk rhyme:

> If you're white, you're right.
> If you're brown, step around.
> If you're black, get back!

Afro-American readers who recognize the echo from their own comic lore enjoy a wry in-joke that others might not see as funny.

Doubtless some critics were just not accustomed to laughing over serious black novels, jokes in the work of, say, Willard Motley or Richard Wright being rare indeed. *The Yale Review's* James Yaffe, for example, extols *Invisible Man's* "tightly effective" "brooding, bitter tone" and its "passages of great sociological interest"; these are virtues one finds in Motley's and Wright's work. But then Yaffe misses the ambitiousness and the comedy of Ellison's project: he lumps what he labels this "crude," "overearnest" novel with others of the season "of little or no humor."[33]

11

Other critics, notably those who had come of age during the thirties era of heightened consciousness, were too aware of the offensiveness of humor relying on ethnic stereotypes not to feel uneasy in the face of Ellison's freewheeling race humor. "By the time I finished *Invisible Man* in the early '50's," says Ellison, "I had white friends, sensitive readers, people who knew much of the world's great literature, reading my novel . . . and reacting as though it were against the law and in utter bad taste for a white reader to laugh at a black character in a ridiculous situation. Only one or two critics were free [enough] of this involvement to say, 'Well, this is very funny.' I intended it to be funny."[34]

In *Invisible Man* Ellison brilliantly exploits this tension over black/white humor. Racial epithets are hurled at Invisible Man by the white men at the battle royal, by Bledsoe, by the doctors in the factory hospital. Tod's dancing Sambo dolls, symbolizing his manipulation by the Brotherhood and prefiguring his suicide, and the stereotypically wide-smiling, blackfaced penny bank at Mary's – both crass images raise the question of the social function of ethnic stereotypes and humor. That Invisible Man cannot get rid of the bulky bank but must carry it with him until the end suggests that, grotesquely distorted as it is, the popular American image – "the black image in the white mind" – nonetheless serves as part of his cultural baggage, part of his identity. Doubtless, too, it stands as a warning to him as he moves out of Mary's with plans to become active in the Brotherhood, where again and again he is viewed as some sort of blacked-up entertainer. "But don't you think he should be a little blacker?" says Emma at the first Brotherhood party (295).

Indeed, the novel's meditation on ethnic laughter takes quite a baffling turn at this same party when "a short broad man," a drunken white man, blurts out that he wants Invisible Man to give the group a song:

> "How about a spiritual, Brother? Or one of those real good ole Negro work songs? Like this: *Ah went to Atlanta – nevah been there befo',*" he sang, his arms held out from his body like a penguin's wings, glass in one hand, cigar in the other. "*White man sleep in a feather bed, Nigguh sleep on the flo'* . . . . Ha! Ha! How about it, Brother?"

12

Brother Jack tells this man that Invisible Man does not sing, and that insisting that he do so (the broad man informs Jack that *"all* colored people sing") "is an outrageous example of unconscious racial chauvinism!" The man is hustled roughly from the room, leaving an "enormous silence" in his wake. Invisible Man suddenly shatters the silence by yelling, "What's the matter with you? Haven't you ever seen a drunk?" Then he breaks into hysterical laughter, and finds that everyone joins in:

> "He hit me in the face." I wheezed. "He hit me in the face with a yard of chitterlings!" . . . . The silent tension of the others was ebbing into a ripple of laughter that sounded throughout the room, growing swiftly to a roar, a laugh of all dimensions, intensities and intonations. Everyone was joining in. . . . Across the room they were pounding someone on the back to keep him from choking. Handkerchiefs appeared, there was much honking of noses, wiping of eyes. A glass crashed to the floor, a chair was overturned. I fought against the painful laughter, and as I calmed I saw them looking at me with a sort of embarrassed gratitude. . . . They smiled. Several seemed about to come over and pound my back, shake my hand. It was as though I had told them something which they'd wished very much to hear, had rendered them an important service which I couldn't understand. But there it was, working in their faces. My stomach ached. I wanted to leave, to get their eyes off me. (304–306)

In this complex scene, the broad man hits Invisible Man with "a yard of chitterlings" by hauling an in-group stereotype (in this case, the joke might be told by whites on blacks, or by blacks spoofing the things whites say about them) into a mixed, public setting. Though expelled from the room, the broad man manages, before leaving, to scapegoat Invisible Man, too: to enforce upon him his pained difference, his profound alienation. Although the protagonist senses that the remaining whites were "about to come over and pound my back, shake my hand," no one does touch him, and the scene nears an end with him under the steady pressure of their terror-filled (alienated) eyes. This encounter contains again a sign of things to come: As "brotherly" as the organization claims to be, it is still infected with racism, which will soon turn against both Invisible Man and Harlem.

Despite the typically Ellisonian storm cloud over this comic scene, the laughter here has a positive side. Significantly, the racial stereotype and Invisible Man's invitation, by his own laughter, of the whites to laugh at it induce a rare moment of shared closeness in the interracial group. The whites are relieved and grateful that the black guest takes no general offense at the broad man's aggressive racial remark. If they do not pound his back or shake his hand, they at least balance their terror with a smile in his direction for not losing his humorous perspective on what has happened and for not thus stirring their guilt. (In a recent interview, Ellison observed wryly that white Americans depend upon blacks' ability to retain an optimistic, or comic, view of life; if blacks can stay optimistic, how bad can things be for everybody else?)[35]

In 1970, Ellison pointed out that this racial and even racist humor, albeit callously reductive, has, ironically, served to help Americans to adjust to one another:

> This is one of the secrets of the power of humor. [It is] a cementing factor, which sometimes humanizes by reducing the outsider, or the opponent, to the level of the ridiculous. But there is something else about humor which makes it very, very tricky. It tends to make us identify with the one laughed at despite ourselves. It seems that in order to have the insight to isolate the comic defect or the aspect within the other person, you have to make the human identification . . . . When Americans can no longer laugh at one another, then they have to fight with one another. The humanizing factor gets lost, and we lose our resiliency, our ability to bend a little bit and to adapt.[36]

In this sense, the broad man's invitation to sing, like the Sambo bank that Invisible Man cannot discard, is, oddly enough, quite a useful part of his cultural equipment; joke target that he is, he will need the ability to laugh at himself, regardless of who else is laughing, or why. Then, too, if only for a fleeting, ambiguous instant, it is a salve and binding force for all present. The strained scene draws out a New England woman, who comes over to Invisible Man to apologize and express understanding. "You are here to fight along with us, not to entertain," she says (306).

More than in-jokes make this book funny. Despite its tragic episodes – and even despite Ellison's statement that he structured the novel according to Kenneth Burke's "tragic rhythm" formula of purpose-passion-perspective (*SA*, 176–7) – *Invisible Man's* basic mode is comedy.³⁷ Even the sad tales of Trueblood and Tod have uproariously funny aspects. The very premise of the novel, that the main character cannot be seen, due to whatever causes, is comical, the comedy serving to balance and even to underscore the extreme seriousness of Ellison's studies of blindness and sight, lightness and darkness, perception and ignorance, being and nothingness, the strange ambiguities and "polarities" of life.³⁸

Invisible Man is not "a smart man playing dumb," as one critic has argued;³⁹ rather, he really *is* dumb, or, more accurately, he is exaggeratedly naive, hilariously so. As Bledsoe and others tell him, he does not even know the difference between the way things are and the way they are supposed to be (a key phrase and juxtaposition for Ellison); or, framed more largely, he does not realize that there is a gaping breach, most particularly for blacks, dividing America's ideals or "sacred documents" (its "principles," his grandfather says) from the way people really do treat one another. This absurdly disjointed space, this no-man's-land through which Invisible Man moves unseen, is fertile ground for the comic: It is the American "land of the free" where Invisible Man, as a black (thus blatantly *un*free), takes orders from Marse Jack and others who set him "running."

Like a slapstick comedian, Invisible Man finds that his efforts to stop being "run" fail conspicuously; indeed, they consistently produce effects in comic opposition to those he intends. His graduation speech, for instance, wins him not respect and glory but humiliation and a mouth full of blood; the scholarship sends him on the downward road to deeper distresses and failures; his attempts to win the white trustee's confidence and patronage earn him instead expulsion from school; his efforts to lead his people toward brotherhood lead to his betraying Harlem and helping to spark a community-destroying (and, we should add in his defense, purifying) race riot. In some ways he is a Charlie Chaplin clown figure, "skidding around corners and dashing down alleys, endlessly hurrying in search of whatever it is that can sanctify human existence."⁴⁰ He is the ever-ready butt of practical jokers' wiles: The smoker, the letters from Bledsoe, the note from dog-faced Jack, with his weird, secret smiles may be viewed as peculiarly vicious play of this sort. These initiatory incidents season him for a society

15

of violently quick changes, phony appearances, disappointments, and foul caprice. As such an uncautious dupe, Invisible Man stands in a very long line of American innocents, earnest seekers of success who find their faces in the dust.

Invisible Man's memoirs are framed as a tall tale, or, as Ellison once put it, as an "exalted lie."[41] The novel's first sentence, indeed the entire prologue, places the reader in the once-upon-a-time world of the tall tale or the lie. And several of the novel's speakers – Trueblood and Tarp, for example – have their say in the high-spiritedly hyperbolic terms of this folk form. When Ras spurs his "hoss" through riot-hot Harlem, certain hard-drinking observers lampoon the scene in "exalted liarly" style:

> "This is some night," one of them said. "Ain't this some night?"
> "It's 'bout like the rest."
> "Why you say that?"
> " 'Cause it's fulla fucking and fighting and drinking and lying – gimme that bottle."
> "You know that stud Ras the Destroyer? Well, man, he was spit-ting blood."
> "That crazy guy?"
> "Hell, yes, man, he had him a big black hoss and a fur cap and some kind of old lion skin or something over his shoulders and he was raising hell. Goddam if he wasn't a sight, riding up and down on this ole hoss, you know, one of the kind that pulls vegetable wagons, and he got him a cowboy saddle and some big spurs."
> (549)

When a cop starts to shoot at him, "Ole Ras didn't have time to git his gun so he let fly with that spear and you could hear him grunt and say somthing 'bout that cop's kinfolks and then him and that hoss shot up the street leaping like Heigho, the goddam Silver!" (549–52).

Here the storyteller's voices and the mix of cultural artifacts and modes – "the beautiful absurdity of their American identity"[42] – are comic: the West Indian with an Eastern title of authority, Ras; his yelling "something in African or West Indian or something"; the vegetable wagon nag; the Hollywood spear; the Lone Ranger-like gunplay. As serious and dangerous as Ras may be, Ellison shares with his reader the joke of how funny "Ole Ras" really does look and sound. The joke here is vintage Ellison: that whatever else Ras might be, he is in many ways prototypically American in his comic efforts to improvise a style with which to face the deadly but still funny streets of New York. In this respect, Ras is an odd twin of Invisible Man himself, confusedly struggling to figure out who he is and to take his stand against Harlem's badmen.

Not only is *Invisible Man* a novel replete with comic moments and characters; the protagonist learns, throughout the course of the book, to adopt a comic attitude toward life. In a sense, he learns to do what his grandfather has said was necessary: to "undermine 'em with grins." In the book's final sections he sees at last that he lives in an absurdly shifting world, an off-balance place on the brink of disaster where one vitally needs the capacity not only to "laugh to keep from crying" but to be ready to act creatively under pressure. In his funeral sermon for Tod — one of the book's several unforgettable speeches — Invisible Man tells the crowd that Tod's "blood ran like blood in a comic-book killing, on a comic-book street in a comic-book town on a comic-book day in a comic-book world" (446). The tragic loss of Tod (one mourner's placard reads, "Our Hope Shot Down") and the maddeningly brazen activities of Rev. Rinehart-the-Rascal drive home to Invisible Man the true nature of the "comic-book" American experience. "How had I missed it for so long?" he muses. "Hadn't I grown up around gambler-politicians, bootlegger judges and sheriffs who were burglars; yes, and Klansmen who were preachers and members of humanitarian societies?" (499). As by slow degrees he perceives the prevalence of comic circumstances in "The United States of Jokeocracy,"[43] he also sees that time and again he has been treated not like a man but like an object, which treatment Henri Bergson has termed the essence of the comic.[44] Invisible Man eventually sees that for Norton, Emerson, Jack, and the others, "I was simply a material, a natural resource to be used" (497).

To face this situation, Invisible Man arms himself, as the "timbre" of his narrative voice proves, with an unrelentingly comic frame of reference, one that is neither sentimental nor cynical. "The comic frame," writes Kenneth Burke,

> in making a man a student of himself, makes it possible for him to "transcend" occasions when he has been tricked or cheated, since he can readily put such discouragements in the assets column, un-

der the head of "experience." . . . In sum, the comic frame should enable people to be observers of themselves, while acting. Its ultimate would not be passiveness, but *maximum consciousness.* One would "transcend" himself by noting his own foibles.[45]

It is from this deeply comic perspective that Invisible Man, nearing the end of the book-long series of painful lessons, can eloquently proclaim:

> And now all past humiliations became precious parts of my experience, and for the first time, leaning against that stone wall in the sweltering night, I began to accept my past and, as I accepted it, I felt memories welling up within me. It was as though I'd learned suddenly to look around corners; images of past humiliations flickered through my head and I saw that they were more than separate experiences. They were me; they defined me. I was my experiences and my experiences were me, and no blind men, no matter how powerful they became, even if they conquered the world, could take that, or change one single itch, taunt, laugh, cry, scar, ache, rage or pain of it. (497).

Burke makes it clear that the comic perspective permits one to be flexible enough to face life's unpredictable changes, and despite them to be optimistically poised to respond effectively. By viewing the world comically, not only can Invisible Man "grin 'em to death," but he can also nurture his own life, taking all things, however absurdly baffling, as they come. For the reader, too, the novel's comedy carries a variety of lessons: It recalls Ellison's formula that "the antidote to *hybris,* to overweening pride, is irony, that capacity to discover and systemetize clear ideas";[46] it also generates the capacity not only to mock but to identify with this man so low down on society's hierarchy that he has dropped from sight.

In an essay entitled "The Little Man at Chehaw Station," Ellison defines at length the predicament of the American artist vis-à-vis his audience.[47] It is not enough, he states, for the writer to write "just for himself" or, worse, just for critics or for those of privileged backgrounds. His point is that in any American audience, chances are that "the little man" is there, both as collaborator and as ruthless judge. "The little man" is Ellison's metaphor for the member of the American audience who arises from the lower depths of the social hierarchy steeped in vernacular experience but widely travelled, intellectually and culturally, and very much at home in the world of the art forms that he prefers. Indeed, all humble appearances notwithstanding, his knowledge and taste may not only complement but surpass the artist's own. Thus the artist's challenge is not just to make the best art possible, always and everywhere, but to remember the little man's taste for American vernacular as well as for imported or highbrow materials. Perhaps the artist's still more trying challenge is to seek to demonstrate the connections, however snarled or makeshift they may be, between the little man (Trueblood or Tarp, for example, or Invisible Man himself) and his more affluent countrymen (Norton, say, or Emerson).

As he wrote his novel, Ellison certainly knew that among his readers would be those who have never met a Trueblood, a Tarp, or an Invisible Man. Such readers, Ellison has pointed out, present the writer with "a basic problem of rhetoric":

> How does one in the novel . . . persuade the American reader to identify that which is basic in man beyond all differences of class, race, wealth, or formal education? How does one . . . make the illiterate and inarticulate eloquent enough so that the educated and more favorably situated will recognize wisdom and honor and charity, heroism and capacity for love when found in humble speech and dress?[48]

Ellison's "rhetoric" reaches out to express all of his characters' robust humanity. But this writer makes no artistic compromises, offers no bent-over-backward pleas for sympathy. Indeed, one factor explaining Ellison's phenomenal success in writing a classic the first time out is that he had his eye fixed not so much on the "educated and more favorably situated" reader as on the little man.

Bursting with vernacular forms growing out of black American experience — most strikingly the comic forms — this novel is anything but folk art. Yet, as several critics have pointed out, it is a work that is rooted in the vernacular. Albert Murray calls the novel "par excellence the literary extension of the blues. It was," continues Murray, "as if Ellison had taken an everyday twelve bar blues tune (by a man from down South sitting in a manhole up North in New York signifying about how he got there) and scored it for full orchestra. . . . It had new dimensions of rhetorical resonance (based on lying and signifying)."[49] By reaching that unlikely sophisticate, the largely self-taught "little man at Chehaw Station," Ellison was also able to reach an extraordinarily wide audience, including those from backgrounds quite unlike his own or his characters' but who identified themselves with the ranging style of Ellison's projected "little" collaborator. By stepping through "the narrow door of the particular,"[50] as Nathan Scott put it, Ellison arrived at the universal; by tickling the funnybone of his own folks from back home, he arrived at what Henry James called "the country of the blue" − or, if you will, the country of the blues.

NOTES

1. Ralph Ellison and John Hersey, "Introduction: 'A Completion of Personality,'" in *Ralph Ellison, A Collection of Critical Essays*, ed. John Hersey (Englewood Cliffs, N.J.: Prentice-Hall, 1974), p. 19.

2. F. W. Dupee, "On 'Invisible Man,'" *Book Week (The Washington Post)*, September 26, 1965, p. 4.

3. R. W. B. Lewis, "Eccentrics' Pilgrimage," *The Hudson Review*, 6 (1953):44.

4. See, for example, Robert Bone, "Ralph Ellison and the Uses of Imagination," in *Anger and Beyond*, ed. Herbert Hill (New York: Harper & Row, 1966), pp. 86–111; and Edward Margolies, "History as Blues," in *Native Sons, A Critical Study of Twentieth Century Negro American Authors* (Philadelphia: Lippincott, 1968, 1969), pp. 127–48.

5. Alice K. Turner, "'Invisible Man' At Thirty," *The Nation*, 1 (May 1982):529.

6. Lewis, "Eccentrics' Pilgrimage," p. 148.

7. Albert Murray, *The Omni-Americans* (New York: Outerbridge and Dienstfrey, 1970), p. 167.

8. For insight into the process of canonization, I am indebted to my colleague, Richard M. Ohmann. See his "The Social Definition of Literature" in *What Is Literature*, ed. Paul Hernadi (Bloomington: Indiana University Press, 1978), pp. 89–101.

9. "The World Below," *The New York Times Book Review*, 13 (April 1952), p. 5.

10. "Fiction Chronicle: The Wrongs of Innocence and Experience," *Partisan Review*, 19 (May–June 1952):359.

11. Dupee, "On 'Invisible Man,'" p. 4.

12. *The Negro History Bulletin*, 17, (October 1953):20 [unsigned book review].
13. Jonathan Yardley, "30 Years on the 'Raft of Hope,'" *The Washington Post*, April 1982, p. B6.
14. For a good sampling of critical works on *Invisible Man*, see *Ralph Ellison: A Collection of Critical Essays*, ed. John Hersey (Englewood Cliffs, N.J.: Prentice-Hall, 1974); and *Twentieth Century Interpretations of Invisible Man*, ed. John Reilly (Englewood Cliffs, N.J.: Prentice-Hall, 1970).
15. The references to Shaw and James are not by chance. Among Ellison's earliest discoveries, long before it had occurred to him to try to become a writer, was an edition of Shaw's plays; he learned a great deal from the playwright's prefaces and later tried, in his first published essays, to strike something of a Shavian note. In the thirties, Richard Wright directed Ellison to a collection of Henry James' prefaces, which proved an even more important instructive source.
16. See Abner W. Berry, "Ralph Ellison's Novel 'Invisible Man' Shows Snobbery, Contempt for Negro People," *The Worker*, 1 (June 1952):7.
17. Roi Ottley, "Blazing Novel Relates a Negro's Frustrations," *The Chicago Tribune*, May 1952, p. 4; on this question of the representativeness of black characters, see Sterling Brown, "Our Literary Audience," *Opportunity*, 8 (February 1930):42–6, 61.
18. *The Saturday Review*, October 24, 1964, p. 60.
19. Houston A. Baker, *Blues, Ideology, and Afro-American Literature* (Chicago: University of Chicago Press, 1984), pp. 172–99.
20. Ralph Ellison, *Shadow and Act* (New York: Random House, 1964), p. 59. This volume will hereafter be cited as *SA*.
21. "Ralph Ellison Explains," *'48 Magazine of the Year*, 2 (May 1948):145.
22. Ralph Ellison, Steve Cannon, Lennox Raphael, and James Thompson, "A Very Stern Discipline," *Harper's Magazine*, March 1967, p. 84.
23. Ralph Ellison, "Society, Morality, and the Novel," in *The Living Novel*, ed. Granville Hicks (New York: Macmillan, 1957), p. 69.
24. Ralph Ellison and John Hersey, from an interview in *I Speak for You*, ed. Kimberly Benston (Washington, D.C.: Howard University Press, forthcoming).
25. Vigot Sjoman, "*En Val Synlig Man,*" *Dagens Nyeter*, 3 (January, 1955):4.
26. Dupee, "On 'Invisible Man,'" p. 4.
27. See Lloyd L. Brown, "The Deep Pit," *Masses and Mainstream*, 5 (June

1952):62–4; Ernest Kaiser, "A Critical Look at Ellison's Fiction and at Social and Literary Criticism By and About the Author," *Black World*, 20 (December 1970):53–9, 81–97; Addison Gayle, *The Way of the New World: The Black Novel in America*, (Garden City, N.Y.: Double-day, 1975).

28. In 1954, Ellison told his Salzburg seminar students that his novel actually was written for blacks: "There are lots of little things, sayings and folklore, that whites can't really understand." Sjoman, "En Val," p. 4.

29. "Introduction by Ralph Ellison" to *Romare Bearden: Paintings and Projections* (State University of New York at Albany: The Art Gallery, 1968); reprinted in Ellison, *Going to the Territory* (New York: Random House, 1986).

30. Ralph Ellison, *Invisible Man* (New York: Random House, 30th Anniversary Edition, 1952, 1982), p. 253. This volume will hereafter be cited as *IM*.

31. This phrase is from Ellison's "Author's Note" prefacing "Out of the Hospital and Under the Bar," which formed part of *Invisible Man's* original text but which finally was cut from the book. "For those who desire more than the sheer narrative ride, who hunger and thirst for 'meaning,'" wrote Ellison, "let them imagine what this country would be without its Marys. Let them imagine, indeed, what the American Negro would be without the Marys of our ever-expanding Harlems. Better still, since fiction is always a collaboration between writer and reader, let them take this proffered middle, this *agon*, this passion, and supply their own beginning, and if an ending, a moral, or a perception is needed, let them supply their own. For me, of course, the narrative is the meaning." *Soon, One Morning*, ed. Herbert Hill (New York: Knopf, 1968), pp. 243–4.

32. "A Special Message to Subscribers from Ralph Ellison," *Invisible Man* (Franklin Center, Pa.: The Franklin Library, 1952, 1980).

33. "Outstanding Novels," *The Yale Review*, 41 (Summer 1952):8.

34. "American Humor" in "Comic Elements in Selected Prose of James Baldwin, Ralph Ellison and Langston Hughes," unpublished thesis by Elwyn E. Breaux, Fisk University, 1971, pp.154–5.

35. Lynn Darling, "Ralph Ellison, the Quiet Legend," *The Washington Post*, April 1982, p. B3. For advice on reading this scene in *Invisible Man*, I am indebted to my colleague Richard Slotkin.

36. Breaux, "American Humor," pp. 152–3.

37. See Kenneth Burke, *A Grammar of Motives* (New York: Prentice-Hall,

1954), pp. 264ff.; and Francis Fergusson, *The Idea of a Theater* (Princeton, N.J.: Princeton University Press, 1949), p. 18.

38. See Kenneth Burke, *Attitudes Toward History* (Boston: Beacon Press, 1937, 1959), p. 18; Burke makes reference to the crucial "Compensation" (1843) of Ralph Waldo Emerson, reprinted in *Emerson: Lectures and Essays* (New York: The Library of America, 1983). pp. 283–301.

39. Stanley Edgar Hyman, *The Promised End* (Cleveland: World Publishing, 1963), pp. 295–315.

40. Lewis, "Eccentrics' Pilgrimage," p. 148.

41. Ellison used this term at a Harvard conference on the contemporary novel held August 4, 1953.

42. The Invisible Man uses this phrase to describe his feelings about "the Jacks and the Emersons and the Bledsoes and Nortons"; *Invisible Man*, p. 546.

43. See Ralph Ellison, "It Always Breaks Out," *Partisan Review*, 30 (Spring 1963):16.

44. Henri Bergson, *Laughter, An Essay on the Meaning of the Comic* (New York: Macmillan, 1937).

45. Burke, *Attitudes*, p. 170.

46. From Ellison's unpublished "Address at Harvard's Alumni Meeting," June 12, 1974.

47. *The American Scholar*, 47 (Winter 1977–8):25–48.

48. "Society, Morality, and the Novel," p. 91.

49. Murray, *Omni-Americans*, p. 167.

50. *Harvard Guide to Contemporary American Writing*, ed. Daniel Hoffman (Cambridge, Mass.: Harvard University Press, 1979), p. 298; Scott cites Cleanth Brooks, "Irony as a Principle of Structure," in *Literary Opinion in America*, ed. Morton Dauwen Zabel (New York: Harper, 1951), p. 729.

2

The Meaning of Narration in
Invisible Man

VALERIE SMITH

1

IN Ralph Ellison's essays and interviews, the artist is a figure of
rebellion. Whether writing generally of the role and responsibilities of the contemporary American novelist or, more specifically, of his own achievements, Ellison describes the artist always
in opposition to the restraints of received literary convention. In
"Brave Words for a Startling Occasion," his acceptance speech for
the 1953 National Book Award, he identifies some of the re-
strictions that limit modern American fiction. For him, neither the
"tight, well-made Jamesian novel" nor the "hard-boiled novel"
can contain the complexity of American life. He writes:

> There was also a problem of language, and even dialogue, which,
> with its hard-boiled stance and its monosyllabic utterance, is one of
> the shining achievements of twentieth-century American writing.
> For despite the notion that its rhythms were those of everyday
> speech, I found that when compared with the rich babel of idi-
> omatic expression around me, a language full of imagery and ges-
> ture and rhetorical canniness, it was embarrassingly austere.[1]

In response to these constraints, he suggests that the contemporary
novelist assume an adversarial posture; he or she must "challenge
the apparent forms of reality – that is, the fixed manners and
values of the few, and . . . struggle with it until it reveals its mad,
vari-implicated chaos, its false faces, and . . . until it surrenders its
insight, its truth" (*SA*, 106).

Likewise, in his famous rebuttal to Irving Howe's "Black Boys
and Native Sons," entitled "The World and The Jug" (1963–4),
Ellison describes his objections to the kind of protest fiction produced by Richard Wright and endorsed by Howe and other critics

25

and reviewers. Finding such representations of black life inordinately bleak, more sociological than literary, he defends his right to create novels that "celebrate human life and therefore are ritualistic and ceremonial at their core. Thus they would preserve as they destroy, affirm as they reject" (*SA*, 114). Locating himself in the tradition of American literary craftsmen and moral writers like Twain, Faulkner, Hemingway, and T. S. Eliot, he denies his intellectual links with and debt to earlier black writers.

The assumptions behind Ellison's formulations have jeopardized his credibility with more ideological writers and scholars. Black aestheticians such as Addison Gayle, Jr., argue that by emphasizing the unversality of his work and vision, Ellison eschews the specific political responsibilities of the black writer.[2] Offering a more subtle indictment, Donald B. Gibson demonstrates that although Ellison denies the political implications of his work, *Invisible Man* is nonetheless "a social document that supports certain values and disparages or discourages others, and as such it must take its place among other forces that seek to determine the character of social reality."[3] Perhaps most generously, Houston A. Baker, Jr., shows that although in his essays Ellison favors the tradition of Western literary art over folklore, his novel actually breaks down the distinction between the two modes of creative discourse and celebrates the black expressive tradition.[4]

The politics of Ellison's rhetoric of rebellion are obviously murky, too complicated to untangle here. His critical writing is replete with images of struggle, subversion, inconoclasm; yet he defends a dissociation of art from politics that is arguably reactionary. I share Baker's sense of the complex relation between the ideology of the essays and the novel. But I would suggest that in at least one way the essays may inform our reading of the fiction: The character of the artist in Ellison's nonfiction corresponds to the portrait of the protagonist of *Invisible Man*.

More than just a failed college student, factory worker, and public speaker, Ellison's invisible man is also an artist. His product: the novel that presents itself as a "simulated autobiography."[5] My analysis will show that like the artist figure in the essays, the fictional protagonist uses his literary talent to subvert his subordinate relation to figures of authority, to expand the overly re-

26

strictive conceptions of identity that others impose upon him. As Ellison himself has often remarked, the novel is in no way the story of his own life.[6] Yet, onto his protagonist he projects his own sense of the artist's power and responsibility. His characterization of the writer in his nonfiction can thus provide terms by means of which we may assess the power and development of the invisible man.

One might describe the story of Ellison's protagonist as the quest for an appropriate identity. Throughout his life he encounters figures of authority — Norton, Bledsoe, the Brotherhood — who impose false names or unsuitable identities upon him. His experiences teach him that the act of naming is linked inextricably to issues of power and control. When he attempts to live according to the dictates of others, he loses his automony and suffers repeated betrayals. He discovers the true meaning of his life only after he assumes responsibility for naming himself by telling his own story.

By linking the narrative act to the achievement of identity, Ellison places his protagonist in a tradition of Afro-American letters that originated with the slave narratives of the late eighteenth and nineteenth centuries. Although these earlier texts were written, at least in part, to generate funds for and interest in the abolitionist cause, they also enabled the writers to name themselves before a culture that had denied their full humanity. When the slave narrators wrote the story of their lives, they seized symbolic authority over themselves from their masters in the South who considered them only partly human. The grandson of emancipated slaves, the invisible man enjoys privileges unavailable to his ancestors in bondage. His ostensible freedom notwithstanding, he is subject to subtler, more pernicious forms of injustice and oppression. He, too, then, employs the narrative process in his search for liberation.

2

The narrator's dying grandfather, a half-mad war veteran, and his college president all warn him in his youth that since the world deceives, he must learn to be deceptive. Speaking in elliptical paradoxes to express an ostensibly self-contradictory message, the

grandfather advises his family to follow his example and undermine the system while pretending to uphold it:

> "I want you to overcome 'em with yeses, undermine 'em with
> grins, agree 'em to death and destruction, let 'em swoller you till
> they vomit or bust wide open. . . . Learn it to the younguns." (16)

Dr. Bledsoe attributes his success to a similar ability to feign humility. Astonished by the young protagonist's ignorance of "the difference between the way things are and the way they're supposed
to be" (139), Bledsoe shares the grandfather's belief in duplicity as
a necessary precondition for achievement. Likewise, the veteran
recognizes the world's deceptions. He, too, tells the protagonist
that he must recognize pretense and learn to be duplicitous:

> . . . learn to look beneath the surface. . . . Come out of the fog,
> young man. And remember you don't have to be a complete fool in
> order to succeed. Play the game, but don't believe in it – that much
> you owe yourself. . . . Learn how it operates, learn how you oper-
> ate. (151)

The invisible man trivializes this recurring lesson until he suffers
repeatedly the consequences of trusting others too readily. As early
as the battle royal, he deludes himself into thinking that he is
shrewd enough to play whatever game is required of him without
believing in it. As if to belie his supposed worldliness, however, his
undertakings backfire and reveal him for the bumpkin he is. When
Emerson shows him Bledsoe's letter, the protagonist seems to realize that he must be skeptical about the way things appear. This
recognition proves to be short-lived, however, because the invisible man soon becomes as devoted to the Brotherhood and its
platform as he was to the American dream and the myth of racial
uplift as embodied by his college. Only after Tod Clifton is murdered, and he recognizes the Brotherhood's complicity in the
Harlem riot, does he understand just how false a face the world
presents.

Feigning sophistication, the invisible man says, for example,
that he doesn't believe in the principles he articulates in his valedictory address, "that humility [is] the secret, indeed, the very
essence of progress" (17). He thinks he only believes that the
semblance of humility works. The embarrassments he suffers in
the battle royal, in college, and in New York show, however, that

he lacks sufficient irony about himself and about the nature of authority to distinguish between what "is" and what "works." Lacking any alternative values he may call his own, he invests more of himself in the principles he espouses than he realizes.

The protagonist displays none of his avowed skepticism at the time of the battle royal. To him, the opportunity to speak before "a gathering of the town's leading white citizens" is unparalleled — "a triumph for [the whole black] community." He expects that the occasion will be somber and dignified, and that once he delivers his oration, the audience will "judge truly [his] ability" (25) and reward him. The scenario the protagonist envisages reveals his sense that his speech, his polish, and his talent have rendered him superior to his peers. But the actual episode resembles only in its basic outline the one that the protagonist anticipates.

The "gathering" turns out to be a bacchanalia. He finds that several black boys his age have been invited to the affair to fight each other; his oratorical skills notwithstanding, he is expected to fight with the others for the audience's entertainment. During the course of the evening the young men are made to watch a nude white woman dance, to fight each other blindfolded, and to dive for counterfeit gold coins on an electrified rug. Each ordeal is designed for their mockery. Yet the invisible man hardly recognizes the disparity between his expectations and the actual situation. He resents fighting in the battle royal not because the match itself is degrading, but because he is repelled by the notion of being lumped together with the other black boys. He fears that the association will "detract from the dignity of [his] speech" (17).

When the white guests ask him to speak at the end of the evening, the protagonist is as determined to impress them as he was when he first arrived at the hotel. Without a second thought, he resolves to recite every word and to observe each intonation as he had practiced them. His meticulous delivery and posture are at least out of place, if not entirely ludicrous, directed as they are at a noisy and disrespectful crowd. But the protagonist is so convinced of the "rightness of things" (30) that he does not even risk offending his audience by spitting out his bloody, salty saliva. The mere possibility of a reward justifies any insults and indignities to which he may be subjected.

The invisible man might have learned from the battle royal episode to mistrust appearances, since the riotous scene of which he was a part bears little relation to the ceremony he had expected. He might have begun to suspect the power elite at large because his audience treated him rudely. But the briefcase and scholarship he receives for delivering his speech eclipse all the earlier unpleasantness. They confirm his assumption that if he does what the world expects of him, he will be rewarded with respect and acceptance. This belief in a reliable relation between cause and effect proves that he is neither the artificer nor the skeptic he pretends to be. Were he at all skeptical of the face the world presents, he would have been somewhat dubious about the existence of causal connections. At this point in his life, however, he is fully confident that things are what they appear and that material rewards await the virtuous.

In college he becomes further committed to this version of the American dream. He and his fellow students virtually worship the administrators and trustees, embodiments of the material success that supposedly ensues from hard work and clean living:

> Here upon this stage the black rite of Horatio Alger was performed to God's own acting script, with millionaires come down to portray themselves; not merely acting out the myth of their goodness, and wealth and success and power and benevolence and authority in cardboard masks but themselves, these virtues concretely! Not the wafer and the wine, but the flesh and the blood, vibrant and alive, and vibrant even when stooped, ancient and withered. (109)

Dr. Bledsoe provides an even more consistently visible image of what the students' best efforts may yield. His story typifies the standard rags-to-riches formula: He arrived at the college barefoot, motivated by "a fervor for education," and distinguished himself initially by being "the best slop dispenser in the history of the school" (114).[7] After years of hard work he became not only president of the school, but a nationally prominent leader as well. In the following description, the protagonist betrays his own mythification of Bledsoe and his inability to distinguish between material reward and moral virtue. The passage, conspicuously lacking in irony, juxtaposes achievements with possessions. Political influence, leadership, and Cadillacs are functionally equivalent; moreover, a light-skinned wife ranks as an acquisition along with these other "possessions":

> [Bledsoe] was the example of everything I hoped to be: Influential with wealthy men all over the country; consulted in matters concerning the race; a leader of his people; the possessor of not one, but *two* Cadillacs, a good salary and a soft, good-looking and creamy-complexioned wife. (99)

When he first meets with Bledsoe after returning Norton to campus, the protagonist begins to see that the president's obsequious, meticulous demeanor is but a facade. In a gesture that emblematizes the disjunction between his veneer and his beliefs, Bledsoe instantaneously rearranges his facial expression, replacing rage with placidity, just before entering Norton's room. This quick, apparently effortless change confirms the protagonist's growing suspicion that Bledsoe's legendary humility is not genuine, but only a performance; at base, he is a manipulative, dishonest power monger.

During their second meeting, Bledsoe asks the protagonist why he did not lie to Norton to avoid showing him Trueblood's shack. The protagonist's response betrays his naiveté; he barely knows what the verb "to lie" means. Duplicity is so foreign to him that he cannot formulate a sentence of which he is the subject, "to lie" is the verb, and a white person is the direct object. "Lie, sir? Lie to him, lie to a trustee, sir? Me?" (137).

Upon realizing that Bledsoe intends to break his promise to Norton and punish him, the protagonist completely loses control of himself. He dimly perceives that if Bledsoe can break his promise to a trustee, and reprimand him although he was not at fault, then contradictions and accidents can happen and effects will not always follow from causes. The protagonist does not want to believe that inconsistencies are possible, however. In an almost surreal sequence, he makes himself reinterpret the meaning of his escapades with Norton, Trueblood, the veteran, and Bledsoe. He forces himself to recast the events in such a way that he is responsible for Norton's accident and that his punishment makes sense. He would rather misunderstand his own experience than see it as a lesson about the disjunction between the way things are and the way they are supposed to be.

Just after he learns of his suspension, the protagonist leaves Bledsoe's office and wanders back to his dormitory in a virtual delirium. Symptomatic of his inability to accept Bledsoe's sentence, he vomits outside the administration building and realizes to his horror that the world around him has literally gone out of focus. In order to restore his normal vision, he covers one of his eyes; by partially blinding himself, he is able to make his way back to his room.

This episode corresponds symbolically with the invisible man's response to what becomes his expulsion. His visual distortion provides an emblem of his brief recognition that his actual experiences with Norton and Bledsoe have disconfirmed his expectations. For a moment, he realizes that his expectations may be fulfilled predictably in his imagination, but that the real world operates according to rules that elude him, if indeed it follows any rules at all. But as he covers one eye to avoid seeing double images, so does he consciously deny the distinction between his expectations and reality. He convinces himself that he was at fault and deserves his suspension; he recasts the earlier sequence of events so that they will explain the outcome logically:

> Somehow, I convinced myself, I had violated the code and thus would have to submit to punishment. Dr. Bledsoe is right, I told myself, he's right; the school and what it stands for have to be protected. There was no other way, and no matter how much I suffered I would pay my debt as quickly as possible and return to building my career. (145)

When the protagonist says that he will "pay [his] debt as quickly as possible and return to building [his] career," he assumes that his future success will at least diminish by contrast, if not justify his present suffering. To put it another way, he expects that the passage of time will convert his humiliation into a mere rite of passage. Such a progressive or linear vision of time is fundamental to both the American dream and the myth of racial uplift; moreover, it is the cornerstone upon which the college was founded. Norton tells the protagonist, for example, that the students are his fate. Their accomplishments in the future will validate and render meaningful his past and present efforts:

32

"Through you and your fellow students I become, let us say, three hundred teachers, seven hundred trained mechanics, eight hundred skilled farmers, and so on. That way I can observe in terms of living personalities to what extent my money, my time and my hopes have been fruitfully invested." (45)

As the protagonist exchanges single- for "double-consciousness,"[8] however, he acknowledges the limitations of his temporal construct. It encourages an investment in the opportunities and possibilities of the future at the expense of the lessons of the past. During the narrative he becomes increasingly able to consider his past experience and learn its lessons.[9] Writing his "autobiography" shows clearly that for him retrospection has acquired value. But only after his second major disillusionment does this realization take place.

During his early days in New York City, the protagonist remains deeply convinced of the rightness of linear vision, of following "the path placed before [him]" (144). The patterns of his thinking display his eagerness to think ahead, his reluctance to reflect. He fantasizes about the future, imagining circumstances that will justify his disgrace. However, he avoids thinking about his past. In his room in the Men's House, for instance, he puts aside the Bible because it makes him homesick and he has no time for nostalgia: "This was New York. [He] had to get a job and earn money" (159). Similarly, when he inadvertently remembers his anger at being expelled, he "hastily" (160) blocks it out. Instead of acknowledging his resentment, he conjures up a future that will redeem his humiliation, one in which he will be Bledsoe's assistant:

> In my mind's eye . . . [Bledsoe] was joined by another figure; a younger figure, myself; become shrewd, suave and dressed not in somber garments (like his old-fashioned ones) but in a dapper suit of rich material, cut fashionably, like those of the men you saw in magazine ads, the junior executive types in *Esquire*. (160–1)

The protagonist intends to find a job in New York by observing professional protocol conscientiously. Well-groomed, prompt, and articulate, he expects that he will easily find suitable employment. Ironically, despite his attempt to manipulate his own appearance, it is he, not the prospective employers, who is taken in by appearances. He trusts his letters because of superficial, inconclusive details: He knows that they are about him, and that they are addressed to "men with impressive names" (148). No doubt the watermark and college letterhead make the letters seem all the more trustworthy. But when Emerson shows him the text of the letters, the protagonist is forced to see that their content is radically different from their impressive exterior.

After this revelation, the protagonist recognizes that the values upon which the school was founded, those that Bledsoe ostensibly tried to teach him, are a sham. His efforts to humble himself and find employment have backfired; he realizes that this version of the American dream will never work for him. Once he renounces the goals that betrayed him, the protagonist behaves in freer and more complex ways than he did previously. His behavior during his last visit to the Men's House, for example, symbolizes his new-found spontaneity and his thorough separation from his earlier goals. As he looks around the boarding house lobby, he feels alienated from the upwardly mobile men with whom he had so recently identified himself. He notes, "I now felt a contempt such as only a disillusioned dreamer feels for those still unaware that they dream" (250). By emptying the spittoon over the head of the Baptist preacher he thinks is Bledsoe, he overturns as well the embodiment of his former dreams.

His disillusionment also causes the protagonist to be less defensive about his past. He now tries to consider and learn from his humiliations, instead of running from them. On the way home from Emerson's office, he begins to hum the melody that someone near him whistles. The tune jars his memory and reminds him of the following lyric from his childhood:

> O well they picked poor Robin clean
> O well they picked poor Robin clean
> Well they tied poor Robin to a stump
> Lawd, they picked all the feathers round from Robin's rump
> Well they picked poor Robin clean. (190)

After reconstructing the song, he is able to use its meaning to understand his own situation: He, like "poor Robin," has been "picked . . . clean." Previously he would have denied all knowledge of what he would consider trivialities such as folk rituals and childhood songs; now he admits that they contain lessons that apply to his present condition.

On the morning of his appointment with Emerson, the invisible man refuses to eat pork chops and grits for breakfast because he wants to avoid being identified with "country" tastes. After he reads Bledsoe's letter, however, he realizes that refined tastes will not necessarily get him anywhere; he therefore begins to accept and to follow his impulses more readily. A reversal of the restaurant episode, the scene in which he eats yams indicates his heightened self-acceptance. Buying the yams and eating them publicly illustrates his willingness to savor both the things he enjoys and the memories they conjure up:

> I stopped as though struck up by a shot, deeply inhaling, remembering, my mind surging back, back. At home we'd bake them in the hot coals of the fireplace, had carried them cold to school for lunch; munched them secretly, squeezing the sweet pulp from the soft peel as we hid from the teacher behind the largest book, the *World's Geography*. Yes, and we'd loved them candied, or baked in a cobbler, deep-fat fried in a pocket of dough, or roasted with pork and glazed with the well-browned fat; had chewed them raw – yams and years ago. More yams than years ago, though the time seemed endlessly expanded, stretched thin as the spiraling smoke beyond all recall. (256–7)

The narrator refers to his pre-Brotherhood, postcollege phase as a "period of quietness" (252). He would have done better to call it a "period of inactivity," for although he is unemployed, he does undergo a turbulent period of emotional upheaval during this time. When he could rely on a collectively shared set of values or ethics (like the American dream or the myth of racial uplift), his life was comparatively ordered, and he felt that he ascribed to a system of belief that bestowed upon him a meaningful identity. The intellectual maneuver he performs to make sense of Bledsoe's punishment shows the lengths to which he will go to fit his experiences into a logically explicable context. He appears resilient, if not placid, because he can contain or freeze his emotional responses, like "ice which [his] life had conditioned his brain to produce" (253). His disillusionment (the result of his conversation with Emerson) operates like a "hot red light"; it causes the "ice" to begin to melt and makes it impossible for him to continue to ignore his feelings. The pain of living at such an intense level of self-awareness makes the protagonist especially susceptible to the influence of an organization such as the Brotherhood. Despite his resolutions, the Brotherhood tempts him irresistibly by offering him a system of beliefs that both differs strikingly from the one that deceived him and promises to restore meaning and thus quiet to his life. Its superficial differences notwithstanding, the Brotherhood's ideals prove, of course, to be as unreliable as the American dream.

The invisible man begins to work for the Brotherhood with the same single-minded faith that he brought to his college and to New York. Predictably, his experience with the Brotherhood recapitulates his disaffection with the principles the college embodies. In the Brotherhood (as in college), the invisible man undergoes the ordeal of an undeserved punishment; in both cases he submits, and accommodates himself to the sentence. Both the Brotherhood and the college betray his faith a second time, however; in each case, the second betrayal occasions his final disillusionment.

In order to place his faith unconditionally in the Brotherhood's tenets, the protagonist thinks he will have to forget the sociology and economics he learned in college (297). In fact, he has to unlearn much more than that. To adhere to the Brotherhood's principles, he also has to deny virtually all of the lessons that his college and postcollege experiences have taught him. The Brotherhood's assumptions and tactics are sufficiently similar to those the protagonist rejected, that he might have recognized them and saved himself some of this despair. His need for place and for a system of belief is so profound, however, that it blinds him to these resemblances.

The invisible man becomes disaffected with the values Bledsoe represents at least in part because they sacrifice the individual for the system. Considering him utterly insignificant, the college president resolves to destroy the protagonist's career, despite his innocence, in order to save the image of the school. The protagonist finds Bledsoe's logic incomprehensible, if not nonexistent; he therefore distances himself from the traditional American values Bledsoe embodies in order to preserve or create his own identity.

The Brotherhood similarly considers the interests of the individual insignificant in relation to those of the organization, although unlike Bledsoe it admits this bias overtly. As Brother Jack tells the invisible man at their first meeting, "you mustn't waste your emotions on individuals, they don't count" (284). Tempted by the promise of material and intellectual comfort, the protagonist affiliates himself with the group, even though, for him, individuals (himself in particular) do count. Indeed, his subsequent problems with the Brotherhood arise from this difference of opinion. Although he considers it reasonable to follow his own judgment and try to articulate the concerns of the black community, the Brotherhood finds his behavior divisive and censures him.

The protagonist had learned earlier that his own past experiences, as well as folk traditions, could teach him about his present condition. He should therefore have suspected the Brotherhood when it tried to cut him off from his past by changing his name and offering him a "new beginning" (327). But he allows himself to be seduced into the Brotherhood because it provides him with a system of belief that makes individual and political action significant. He cannot resist the hope of finding some meaning in a life and in a world that appear to be chaotic. As he notes in a description of the early days of his Brotherhood career:

> [For] one lone stretch of time I lived with the intensity displayed by those chronic numbers players who see clues to their fortune in the most minute and insignificant phenomena: in clouds; on passing trucks and subway cars, in dreams, comic strips, the shape of dog-luck fouled on the pavements. I was dominated by the all-embracing idea of Brotherhood. The organization had given the world a new shape, and me a vital role. We recognized no loose ends, everything could be controlled by our science. (373)

The protagonist's eagerness to escape his past and begin his life anew dooms him to repeat his earlier mistakes. Understandably, he would like to forget his suffering, humiliation, and cynicism. As he remarks before his first Brotherhood speech, "if I were successful . . . I'd be on the road to something big. No more flying apart at the seams, no more remembering forgotten pains" (327). But when he forgets "his pains," he also loses his ironic perspective on figures of authority and makes himself vulnerable once again to their mistreatment.

Indeed, he consciously stops himself from looking at the organization with any skepticism, as if being in the group but not of it were only disloyal, and not self-protective as well:

> I would have to take that part of myself that looked on with remote eyes and keep it always at the distance of the campus, the hospital machine, the battle royal – all now far behind. Perhaps the part of me that observed listlessly but saw all, missing nothing, was still the malicious arguing part; the dissenting voice, my grandfather part; the cynical, disbelieving part – the traitor self that always threatened internal discord. Whatever it was, I knew that I'd have to keep it pressed down. (327)

As a result, he does not (or will not) recognize the Brotherhood's mistreatment of him. He is as innocent of Brother Wrestrum's accusations as he was of Bledsoe's. As he did in the president's office, the protagonist initially explodes when he hears of his punishment. But he accommodates himself yet again to the will of his superior so that he will not be forced to question the institution's ideology. He needs so desperately to trust the Brotherhood that he convinces himself that the reprimand and reassignment are signs of their faith in, not their displeasure with, him:

> [After] all, I told myself, the assignment was also proof of the committee's goodwill. For by selecting me to speak with its authority on a subject which elsewhere in our society I'd have found taboo, weren't they reaffirming their belief both in me and in the principles of Brotherhood, proving that they drew no lines even when it came to women? They had to investigate the charges against me, but the assignment was their unsentimental affirmation that their belief in me was unbroken. (398)

The sequence of events that culminates in Tod Clifton's murder precipitates the invisible man's thorough and lasting reexamination of himself and his relation to authority and ideology. When he sees Clifton selling Sambo dolls on the street corner, the protagonist assumes that he must have been mad to leave the Brotherhood (ostensible order and meaning) for such a degrading and meaningless endeavor: "Why should a man deliberately plunge out of history and peddle an obscenity?" he asks himself. "Why should he choose to disarm himself, give up his voice and leave the only organization offering him a chance to 'define' himself?" (428). As he considers the nature of Clifton's wares and the fact of his death, however, the protagonist begins to question this formulation. He considers what he and the Brotherhood mean by "history" and acknowledges that the record in which they jointly believe is selectively and arbitrarily preserved; the Brotherhood's ideology is, therefore, no more sacrosanct than any other. Moreover, he begins to question the significance of blacks as a race within the Brotherhood's historical construct, given that its spokesmen persistently deny the importance of race as a category of distinction. The sight of other young blacks causes him to realize that his devotion to the Brotherhood has alienated him from the needs of his people. He remarks that Clifton "knew them better" (432) than he; presumably, his inability to reconcile the people's needs with the Brotherhood's forced him to abandon the organization. Once he perceives that the Brotherhood has ignored the interests of the race, it becomes clear (although it is not explicitly stated in the text) that Clifton's Sambo dolls are not randomly selected products to be hawked on the streets. The black caricatures dangled on a string are, instead, metaphors for the black members of the Brotherhood who are manipulated, unknowingly, by the white leadership.

The invisible man plans a public funeral for Clifton in hopes of organizing the black community in response to a particularly sensitive incident: the shooting of an unarmed black man by a policeman. The construction he puts on Clifton's murder differs markedly from the Brotherhood's because he places such a premium on the fact of race. For the protagonist, it is more politically significant that Clifton was black than it is that he was a defector. In addition, he is more concerned with organizing the black community than he is with preserving the integrity of the Brotherhood's reputation. The Brotherhood spokesman, in contrast, see Clifton's death primarily as the murder of a traitor: an event that concerns them only minimally. They therefore rebuke the protagonist for organizing a hero's funeral. To their minds, faithfulness to the Brotherhood's cause outweighs race as a consideration.

The Brotherhood's response to Clifton's death and funeral confirms the invisible man's worst fears about the organization.[10] Within the Brotherhood, he is as invisible as he was in his hometown and at his college. He is significant to Brother Jack and the other leaders only to the extent that he effectively and obediently articulates the party line. Outside of his narrowly defined role within the organization, he does not exist for them. He had mistakenly thought that by upholding the Brotherhood's ideology, he would find purpose and meaning for his life. Clifton's death and his reprimand show him, however, that his life will derive meaning from the platform only if he renounces the prior claims of his own judgment, his own priorities, and, incidentally, his own race. To put it another way, he will have an identity in the Brotherhood only if he concedes the possibility of creating the meaning of his life for himself.

The protagonist's mistrust of the Brotherhood precipitates a time of reflection for him. This betrayal reminds him of the other people who have betrayed him in similar ways. Like Norton and Bledsoe, Jack and others treat him as if he does not exist. Each man needs to think of him in a certain way, and thus sees only the image he projects:

> Here I had thought [the Brotherhood] accepted me because they felt that color made no difference, when in reality it made no difference because they didn't see either color or men. . . . [All the people who betrayed him] were very much the same, each attempting to force his picture of reality upon me and neither giving a hoot in hell for how things looked to me. I was simply a material, a natural resource to be used. (497)

His betrayal also prompts him to remember his grandfather's admonition; as he did at the beginning of the narrative, he resolves at the end as well to undercut the game (this time the Brotherhood's) even as he pretends to play it.

He reverts to his earlier attempt at duplicity, at least in part, because he discovers accidentally that he can manipulate his appearance to his own advantage. Afraid of being recognized and beaten by Ras the Exhorter's followers, the protagonist dons sunglasses and a hat, only to find that all of Harlem now thinks that he is Rinehart, the quintessential hustler. He realizes that if he changes his appearance just a bit, he is able to circumvent the problems of being himself and to enjoy the benefits of being someone else.

The invisible man's betrayals have caused him to believe that no institution, no ideology, is wholly reliable. Given his sense of a chimerical reality, the identity of Rinehart seems to suit him, for Rinehart is a consummate manipulator of surfaces: pimp, numbers runner, lover, and preacher, he is all things to all people. The protagonist finds the idea of a Rinehart appealing on two grounds. First, Rinehart provides him with an identity into which he can escape with ease. Second and more importantly, the invisible man is compelled by the hustler because he is able to change identities at will, thereby turning the ephemeral nature of the world to his advantage. In the following passage, he remarks on the place of a Rinehart figure in a chaotic society:

> What is real anyway?. . . . The world in which we lived was without boundaries. A vast seething, hot world of fluidity, and Rine the rascal was at home. Perhaps *only* Rine the rascal was at home in it. It was unbelievable, but perhaps only the unbelievable could be believed. Perhaps the truth was always a lie. (487)

The protagonist thinks that by following the example of his grandfather (of which Rinehart is an extreme instance) and feigning compliance, he will protect himself from further deceptions and acquire some authority over his own life. This experiment works for a time; he reinstates himself in the Brotherhood's good graces by telling its leaders only those things about Harlem it wishes to hear – that increased numbers of black people are joining the ranks, for example – and generally affecting a submissive demeanor. At the scene of the Harlem riot, however, he discovers that his false acquiescence has backfired. Because the leaders have withheld the full complexity of their platform, he has been implicated in a conspiracy of which he knew nothing. He had intended to organize the black community; instead, he has been involved unknowingly in the Brotherhood's effort to destroy it:

It was not suicide, but murder. The committee had planned it. And I had helped, had been a tool. A tool just at the very moment I had thought myself free. By pretending to agree I had indeed agreed, had made myself responsible for that huddled form lighted by flame and gunfire in the street, and all the others whom now the night was making ripe for death. (541)

As this passage indicates, the invisible man realizes the implausibility of feigning compliance with the dominant ideology. Because he is necessarily subordinate to figures of authority, he will never know the full complexity of their program. Commitment to an ideology requires a leap of faith, a leap he has always been only too willing to make. Yet each time he commits himself, what he "leaps" over threatens to destroy him.

In other words, what he learns ultimately is that he will have no control over his own life if he tries to play the game but not believe in it. As he notes, "[he] had been used as a tool. [His] grandfather had been wrong about yessing them to death and destruction or else things had changed too much since his day" (552). Possibly his grandfather could feign compliance while undercutting the system, but he has repeatedly seen that for him, to comply in part is to comply altogether. He therefore resolves to sever his connections to society, to all of the organizations on which he had relied for self-definition, and accepts responsibility for creating his own identity. After his final conference with Brother Hambro he recognizes that if his life is to have any meaning, it must be the sum of all he had undergone: "I was my experiences and my experiences were me, and no blind men, no matter how powerful they became, even if they conquered the world, could take that or change . . . it" (496–7). When he retreats underground to write his own story, he commits himself to sifting through those experiences and attributing his own meaning to them.

3

By choosing to go underground and compose the story of his life, the invisible man shows that he has exchanged one group of mentors — his grandfather, Bledsoe, and the veteran — for another —

Trueblood and Brother Tarp.[11] Both groups, whether explicitly or implicitly, warned him against being too trusting. But whereas the first emphasized the importance of learning to deceive as he is also deceived, the latter provide models for creating a sense of identity independent of what an organization or a collective set of assumptions requires. Throughout the course of his life, the invisible man learns that he can never quite learn to be deceptive enough. No matter how devious he thinks he is, those who control him always manage to trick and betray him. His efforts to create simultaneously an identity inside and outside of an institution therefore seem doomed to failure. When he decides to write his own story, he relinquishes the meaning generated by other ideologies in favor of one that is primarily self-generated. By designating a beginning and an end to his story, he converts events that threaten to be chaotic into ones that reveal form and significance. He creates for himself a persona that develops, indeed exists, in contradistinction to the images that others projected onto him. Moreover, he inverts his relation to the figures of authority who dominated him in "life." As author/narrator he is able to control the identities of such people as Norton, Bledsoe, and Brother Jack. By presenting them in uncomplimentary ways, he avenges the humiliations they inflicted upon him in life. The double consciousness of simultaneously playing and undermining the game proved implausible. But the solution to the problems of identity and authority can be found in the double consciousness of reliving one's story as both narrator and protagonist.

Brother Tarp and Trueblood both appear to realize that their identity is determined by the sum of complex experiences they have undergone. Each man has a story that defines him over and against the identity that others try to impose or project. Tarp conceives of himself as the protagonist of the story of his prison experience. Because he "said no to a man who wanted to take something from [him]" (378), he spent nineteen years in jail and lost his family and his property. He remained in prison until he was able to break free, at which time he determined that he could make it. The story he tells the invisible man, his inescapable memories, his limp, and the link from his leg iron are all ways in which Tarp keeps his past with him in the present. They remind him that he is still looking for freedom, and they remind him of "what [they're] really fighting against" (379). In other words, they keep ever before him those values that he holds most dear and that give his life meaning.

Jim Trueblood also tells a story about a critical experience that reveals his sense of identity. Although the protagonist meets him at a point in the narrative when he can in no way appreciate what the farmer represents, his decision to write his story hearkens back to Trueblood's tale. [12] Like the protagonist, Trueblood is invisible: No one sees him as he is. Because he has slept with his own daughter, blacks consider him a disgrace and whites think of him as a sort of dirty joke. Although others ostracize and ridicule him, Trueblood asserts his own sense of identity by telling and retelling a tale of his own creation. He acknowledges the complexity and ambiguity of his situation: being both guilty and not guilty of incest. As Selma Fraiberg notes, however, instead of allowing myth (or convention) to determine the meaning of his action, Trueblood refuses "to hide behind the cowardly deceptions that cloak sin; he faces the truth within himself."[13] He understands, as the protagonist comes to learn, that he can control the meaning of his life if he converts his own experiences into a narrative and therefore determines what construction should be placed on them. His well-crafted tale prefigures the protagonist's autobiography, a text that endows with meaning events that seemed random as they were "lived" by imposing artistic form on them.[14]

Before beginning his story, Trueblood assumes the stance of the narrator par excellence: "He cleared his throat, his eyes gleaming and his voice taking on a deep incantatory quality, as though he had told the story many, many times" (53). He sets the stage for a complex and subtle story. In order to create the atmosphere of the evening he slept with Matty Lou, he evokes visual, olfactory, and aural images. On that tranquil, critical night, past and present merged for him; he lay in bed with his wife and daughter, remembering another peaceful time in his life when he lived with an earlier lover in a house on the Mississippi. He recalls hearing the river boats approach and conjures up the scene with fluid, sophisticated imagery. Human and animal world, all the senses, dream and waking life, merge. He analogizes the sound of the distant river boats to the "boss bird" calling the covey together during quail season:

> "I'd be layin' there and it would be quiet and I could hear it comin' from way, way off. Like when you quail huntin' and it's getting dark and you can hear the boss bird whistlin' tryin' to get the covey together again, and he's coming toward you slow and whistlin' soft, cause he knows you somewhere around with your gun. Still he got to round them up, so he keeps on comin'. Them boss quails is like a good man, what he got to do he *do!*" (55)

He captures the sound of the boat nearing the house in terms of a visual image that becomes, in turn, aural, gustatory, and then visual again:

> "[It] sounded like somebody hittin' at you slow with a big shiny pick. You see the pick-point comin' straight at you, comin' slow too, and you can't dodge; only when it goes to hit you it ain't no pick a'tall but somebody far away breakin' little bottles of all kindsa colored glass. . . . Then you hear it close up, like when you up in the second-story window and look down on a wagonful of watermelons, and you see one of them young and juicy melons split open a-layin' all spread out and cool and sweet on top of all the striped green ones like it's waitin' just for you, so you can see how red and ripe and juicy it is and all the shiny black seeds it's got and all. And you could hear the sidewheels splashin' like they don't want to wake nobody up; and us, me and the gal, would lay there feelin' like we was rich folks and them boys on the boats would be playin' sweet as good peach brandy wine." (55)

His use of synesthesia reveals the heightened sensuality of his reminiscences on the night he slept with his daughter. Furthermore, the artistry of his story displays the extent to which he has shaped the experience linguistically. By following the associative patterns of his thoughts, he seems to relive the situation as he first experienced it. However, his tale is anything but spontaneous: His use of imagery indicates that he is self-consciously creating the impression (whether true or not) that the atmosphere of the evening was largely responsible for the act of incest.

Given the sensuality of his ruminations while he lies in bed awake, it seems logical that he would have an erotic dream once he falls asleep. As his dream opens, he has just violated custom and entered a white man's house through the front door. Unintentionally, he proceeds to a large white bedroom and discovers there a white woman dressed in a negligee. Although he tries to escape, she holds him back. The tension of the situation is heightened by the grandfather clock, which strikes faster and faster. When he throws the woman on the bed "to break her holt," the two of them begin to sink into her bed:

> "It's sinkin' down so far I think it's going to smother both of us. Then swoosh! all of a sudden a flock of little white geese flies out of the bed like they say you see when you go to dig for buried money. Lawd! they hadn't no more'n disappeared than I heard a door open and Mr. Broadnax's voice said, "They just nigguhs leave 'em do it.'" (58)

In the next phase of the dream, he runs toward the clock and describes his entry into it in terms suggestive of the sexual act and climax.

In the first phase of the dream, Trueblood transgresses a series of social taboos: He enters the white man's home by the front door and has sexual contact with a white woman. Then the dream landscape changes from the representational to the phantasmagoric. When he awakens, he realizes that his actual situation parallels his dream. In life he has just violated a sexual taboo, albeit incest instead of miscegenation. The presence of his wife in the same bed compounds his horror, just as the ticking of the clock exacerbates the tension in the dream. Furthermore, he acknowledges in life, as well as in the dream, the sexual pleasure he derives from the forbidden act.

As Trueblood narrates the sequence of events that took place after he had relations with his daughter, he heightens the reader's sympathy for him by demonstrating both his willingness to accept responsibility for his sin and his attempt to endure his wife's rage. He describes Kate's fury and his readiness to submit to physical punishment by her hand. He even agrees to leave his family for a while. Eventually, however, he insists on returning to them and facing the consequences of his actions. Moreover, he refuses to allow either his wife or his daughter to abort his child and chases away everyone who tries to stand between him and his family.

During the time Trueblood is away from his family, he tries and fails to explain himself to his minister. But religion cannot accommodate or justify his sin and thus cannot help him make sense of his behavior. He tries to determine on his own the extent of his guilt, turning the incident over in his mind. Eventually he sings the blues; like his narrative itself, the music he creates allows him, finally, to come to terms with what he has done.

The subtly complex narrative Trueblood constructs replaces the reductive, derogatory version that the townspeople tell. According to his story, the ambiance of the evening and the dreams it triggered prompted him to initiate intercourse before he was fully awake. He was therefore not entirely conscious when the encounter began. However, he has sufficient self-respect to assume responsibility for his actions, whether intentional or not. Thus he transforms himself from villain or buffoon to hero by proving simultaneously his innocence and his willingness to accept blame.

Like Trueblood, the invisible man chooses and designs his own identity with great care. He rejects the assumption that his past experiences are meaningless and merely sequential in favor of the belief that, taken together, they make up who he is. In his youth he thought that the past was best put at a distance, that identity could be changed at will, and that it could be defined by one's affiliations. By the time he writes the narrative, however, he realizes that all other-imposed identities are false. One's true identity is the sum of one's experiences; therefore, to deny one's past is to deny oneself:

> It was as though I'd learned suddenly to look around corners; images of past humiliations flickered through my head and I saw that they were more than separate experiences. They were me; they defined me. I was my experiences and my experiences were me, and no blind men, no matter how powerful they became, even if they conquered the world, could take that, or change one single itch, taunt, laugh, cry, scar, ache, rage or pain of it. (496–7)

Telling his story allows him to arrange and recount his experiences in such a way as to display the meaning of his life. The beginning and end he chooses, the recurrent patterns he discloses, refute the prevailing opinion that his life lacks significance and is therefore expendable. He shows through his narrative that there is coherence to his life and method to his humiliations. As he learns the value of increased self-reliance, he develops from naiveté and powerlessness to wisdom and authority.

The invisible man might have selected any incident from his life to open the narrative action of his autobiography. If he had wanted immediately to call his reader's attention to his talents, for example, he might have begun by describing at length the first occasion on which he delivered his valedictory address, his high school graduation. Because he intended the first chapter to create quite a different effect, however, he selected for the first memorable event of the novel one that highlights his naive and overly trusting persona. By essentially beginning the narrative with the juxtaposition of the battle royal against the valedictory address, he calls the reader's attention to his own myopia and his overdependence on others' values. This beginning guarantees the reader's awareness that these shortcomings also cause his subsequent humiliations.

The narrator focuses on his own limitations, at least in part, to justify his susceptibility to betrayal. By revealing certain motifs that attend his humiliations, he further shows that some order infuses his experiences even though he was unable to see it when he "lived" them. For example, as I noted earlier, his betrayal by the Brotherhood recapitulates his betrayal by Bledsoe. The invisible man might have avoided his second deception if he had recognized the techniques of deception and his own credulity from his earlier betrayal. Had he wanted to call the reader's attention to the arbitrariness of his humiliations, he could have presented the story in such a way as to emphasize the differences between the two betrayals. The protagonist would then have appeared to be the powerless victim of random, inexplicable circumstances. He highlights both the predictability of organizations and his own culpability, however, by underscoring the similarities between the college and the Brotherhood.

Recounting his story also allows the protagonist to redress the abuses he suffered and overturn the authority of those who misled him in college and in the Brotherhood.[15] Although he was unable to confront them in life, as author of the narrative he can deflate the images of those who ridiculed or deceived him by characterizing them as buffoons and villains. He presents Norton and Homer Barbee, for example, with no small degree of irony in order to undercut the beliefs they profess.

When he is a student, the invisible man clearly reveres Norton and all that he represents. Rich, shrewd, elegantly attired, and exceedingly well-mannered, Norton embodies everything to which the protagonist aspires. Flattered at having been asked to drive for the trustee, the young man is eager to please, fearful of offending. Characteristically, he expects that if he drives and converses well, he will receive some reward: "Perhaps he'd give me a large tip, or a suit, or a scholarship next year" (38). Indeed, even after the protagonist is suspended, he thinks that Norton will be able to help him if only he can find him. By the time he writes the narrative, of course, he has ceased to believe either that wealthy white benefactors are necessarily virtuous or that institutions like the school can uplift the race.

As if to retaliate against Norton for having misled him, the invisible man subtly but unmistakably impugns the motives behind his philanthropy. Norton thinks that he is primarily impelled to support the school by his wish to commemorate his late daughter's memory. The words the narrator attributes to Norton betray his incestuous attraction to her, however, and imply strongly that his generosity may well be an act of atonement for a sin he fails to recognize. When Norton speaks of his daughter, his tone is more that of a bereaved lover than of a father. In addition, he says that he was never able to believe that she was his own, and he expresses an undefined sense of guilt about her. Taken together, these features of his description disclose his problematic relation to her:

> "[My daughter] was a being more rare, more beautiful, purer, more perfect and more delicate than the wildest dream of a poet. I could never believe her to be my own flesh and blood. Her beauty was a well-spring of purest water-of-life and to look upon her was to drink and drink and drink again. . . . She was rare, a perfect creation, a work of purest art. . . . I found it difficult to believe her my own. . . .
> "She was too pure for life," he said sadly, "too pure and too good and too beautiful. . . . I have never forgiven myself."(42)

Norton's response to Trueblood further indicates that his daughter may well have some sexual appeal for him. He overreacts wildly when he learns that the man has slept with his own daughter and has gone unpunished: "'You did and are unharmed!' he shouted, his blue eyes blazing into the black face with something like envy and indignation" (51). Trueblood's powerful narrative devastates Norton because it forces him to confront his own deeply concealed desires. By juxtaposing Norton's and Trueblood's responses to incest, the narrator reveals the extent of both the trustee's misguidance and the farmer's self-awareness. When the event occurred, the protagonist was so overwhelmed by the white man's image and so worried about his own that he totally misread the situation. He not only overestimated Norton, he also treated Trueblood dismissively. In the narrative he corrects this error in judgment. He deposes Norton as a mentor, and by telling his own tale follows Trueblood's example instead.

The protagonist is likewise overly impressed by the Rev. Homer Barbee, who preaches a sermon on the evening of the Trueblood–Golden Day episode. Having jeopardized his college career, the protagonist is moved to guilty tears by Barbee's address, for it celebrates all that the school represents. The minister reminds the students of the legacy of the Founder: Like the school itself, he sprang up from nothing and dedicated himself to the progress of the race. Moreover, Barbee praises Bledsoe's benevolence and leadership:

> "Your leader has kept his promise a thousandfold. I commend him in his own right, for he is the co-architect of a great and noble experiment. He is a worthy successor to his great friend and it is no accident that his great and intelligent leadership has made him our leading statesman. His is a form of greatness worthy of your imitation. I say to you, pattern yourselves upon him. Aspire, each of you, to some day follow in his footsteps. Great deeds are yet to be performed." (30–1)

At the time he hears the speech, the protagonist feels so ashamed of himself that he is unable to stay for the entire service. The speech has convinced him, for at least a short while, that his error has threatened the entire institution. "I could not look at Dr. Bledsoe now, because old Barbee had me both feel my guilt and accept it. For although I had not intended it, any act that endangered the continuity of the dream was an act of treason'' (132).

But looking back at the episode from the end of the narrative, he realizes that the values Barbee articulates are corrupt. The very way in which he notes the minister's blindness mocks his faith in these principles. Given that the narrator knows at the time he recounts the episode that Barbee is blind, he might have acknowledged that fact when he describes the minister's approach to the lectern. If he had wanted to preserve Barbee's image, he might have introduced his speech with a statement like "His blindness did not detract from the insightfulness of his sermon." Instead, he conceals the fact of his blindness until Barbee has completed his stirring message. He describes his sudden fall to his face and then explains in two abrupt sentences why the minister fell: "For a swift instant, between the gesture and the opaque glitter of his glasses, I saw the blinking of sightless eyes. Homer A. Barbee was blind'' (131). One might argue that he narrates the episode as he does to recapture the sequence of his perceptions. But his motives are more complex than such a reading would suggest. He intends the fall and the disclosure of Barbee's blindness to reflect back on the sermon itself. Although he did not realize it when he heard the speech, he now thinks that Barbee must have been intellectually imperceptive (that is, blind) if he believed what he professes.

Like any autobiographer, the invisible man chooses an ending for his narrative that is logically consistent with the meaning of the story as a whole. As Frank Kermode writes, "the provision of an end, [makes] possible a satisfying consonance with the origins and with the middle."[16] He has constructed the tale of his development from ignorance to knowledge both of the meaning of identity and of the proper relation to the power elite. It is therefore to his advantage to end at a point where he is palpably wiser than he was before. However, the invisible man has given his narrative a cyclical structure. Repeatedly he thinks he has figured out how best to maneuver his way around figures of authority, only to find that his strategy has failed him. The decision to remove himself from society and write his own story thus might represent only one of an interminable list of strategies. However, this last one seems to differ from the earlier attempts, for it appears to require him to depend upon himself for the construction of his identity more than his earlier ventures did. But since the story ends before he reenters society, the reader never knows the degree to which he conforms to institutional expectations once he reenters the world.

By ending where he does, then, the invisible man loads the dice in his own favor – one final advantage to telling his own story. He leaves the reader with his conviction that the double consciousness of being both narrator of and participant in his own story empowers him in a way that his earlier duplicity did not. Had he ended his story later, however, this solution might have proven as unfeasible as his previous attempts at compliance or deceit. The persona of the narrative present (the voice of the Prologue and the Epilogue) may well seem more sophisticated than the protagonist only because he knows where to stop.

NOTES

1. "Brave Words for a Startling Occasion," in Ralph Ellison, *Shadow and Act* (New York, Random House, 1972), p. 103. This volume will hereafter be cited as *SA*.
2. See Gayle, *The Way of the World: The Black Novel in America* (Garden City, N.Y.: Doubleday, 1976), pp. 246–58.
3. Gibson, *The Politics of Literary Expression: A Study of Major Black Writers* (Westport, Conn.: Greenwood Press, 1981), p. 93.
4. Baker, "To Move Without Moving: Creativity and Commerce in Ralph Ellison's Trueblood Episode," in *Black Literature and Literary Theory*, ed. Henry Louis Gates, Jr. (New York: Methuen, 1984), pp. 221–48.
5. Richard Bjornson's term. See his essay, "The Picaresque Identity Crisis," in *The Novel and Its Changing Form*, ed. R. G. Collins (Winnipeg, Canada: University of Manitoba Press, 1972), p. 16.
6. See, for instance, "The Art of Fiction: An Interview," in *Shadow and Act*, p. 167.
7. This incident in Bledsoe's past may well be a parody of Booker T. Washington's "entrance examination" for Hampton Institute, when he swept out a recitation room. See *Up from Slavery* in *Three Negro Classics*, ed. John Hope Franklin (New York: Avon Books, 1965), pp. 56–7.

8. The phrase comes, of course, from W. E. B. Du Bois' landmark work, *The Souls of Black Folk*, in *Three Negro Classics*, p. 215.

9. In Robert O'Meally's words, the invisible man learns that "history moves . . . like a boomerang: swiftly, cyclically, and dangerously. . . . when he is not conscious of the past, he is liable to be slammed in the head with it when it circles back." See his book, *The Craft of Ralph Ellison* (Cambridge, Mass.: Harvard University Press, 1980), p. 103.

10. O'Meally also sees this scene as a turning point in the invisible man's development. See *The Craft*, p. 97.

11. Robert Stepto divides up these mentors rather differently than I. See his *From Behind the Veil* (Urbana, Ill.: University of Illinois Press, 1979), p. 177.

12. Trueblood's function in the novel has been the subject of critical debate. E. M. Kist argues that he is an opportunist, "a comic bumbler who cashes in on his pitiful situation by recounting it with broad irony and folk humor." See "A Langian Analysis of Blackness in Ralph Ellison's *Invisible Man*," *Studies in Black Literature*, 7 (1976): 23. For studies that evaluate Trueblood as a blues artist, see Raymond Olderman, "Ralph Ellison's Blues and *Invisible Man*," *Wisconsin Studies in Contemporary Literature*, 7 (1966):146; George E. Kent, "Ralph Ellison and the Afro-American Folk and Cultural Tradition," in *Ralph Ellison: A Collection of Critical Essays*, ed. John Hersey (Englewood Cliffs, N.J.: Prentice-Hall, 1974), pp. 45–6; and Robert O'Meally, *The Craft*, pp. 86–7.

13. Selma Fraiberg, "Two Modern Incest Heroes," *Partisan Review*, 5–6 (1961):659.

14. O'Meally also notes that Trueblood's tale redeems his "absurd situation." See *The Craft*, pp. 36–7.

15. Stepto also discusses Ellison's demystification of mentor figures in the novel. See *Veil*, pp. 178–83.

16. Frank Kermode, *The Sense of an Ending: Studies in the Theory of Fiction* (New York: Oxford University Press, 1967), p. 17.

3

Frequencies of Eloquence: The Performance and Composition of *Invisible Man*

JOHN F. CALLAHAN

1

IN Ralph Ellison's *Invisible Man,* the narrator is a failed orator. Because he is unable to communicate directly with those he meets in American society, Invisible Man abandons the oral tradition in favor of a "compulsion to put invisibility down in black and white" (439). Yet Invisible Man moves back and forth over frequencies of both the spoken and the written word. After giving up as a speechmaker, he writes an improvisatory, vernacular narrative of utterance. But the Prologue and Epilogue with which he frames his tale reveal a continuing, obsessive pursuit of an audience. In the Prologue he is too hurt and vulnerable to risk intimate address even to readers he cannot see. So he puts on a defiant, sometimes hostile mask of invisibility impenetrable to readers except on his terms. Then, as he writes down his story, he does the tough rhetorical psychological work of creating a resilient, genuine voice. After he has told his story, he feels liberated enough to write an Epilogue. There he converses with readers in an intimate, ironic voice whose democratic eloquence calls us to respond with our own dangerous, courageous, socially responsible verbal acts.

Three decades after the publication of *Invisible Man,* Ellison explores the fluctuating, often ambiguous, sometimes contentious relation between the novel and the oral tradition. He does so in an Introduction that is both a meditation and a tall tale about the birth of *Invisible Man.* In the beginning, there were only Ellison and his protean character's voice. And they faced each other not in friendship but opposition, not in intimacy but confrontation.

Ellison reveals that Invisible Man's passage from the spoken to the written word involved an initial struggle between his voice and Invisible Man's until, in a sustained act of "antagonistic co-operation,"[1] Invisible Man performed and he composed the novel. Earlier, Ellison observed that "although *Invisible Man* is *my* novel, it is really his memoir."[2] Now, still the trickster, he writes his Introduction as a factual and fictional, interpretive response to Invisible Man's last call: "Who knows but that on the lower frequencies, *I* speak for *you?*" (439; my emphasis).

Thirty-seven years after Invisible Man announced his presence, Ellison identifies the improvisational beginnings of his form. As he tells it, Invisible Man intruded on him in a barn in Vermont during the summer of 1945 while he was "on sick leave from service in the merchant marine" (ix). Attempting to identify the interloper, Ellison found "nothing more substantial than a taunting disembodied voice" (xiv) who cried out without preliminaries: "I am an invisible man." The upstart voice compelled Ellison to stop writing and listen. "Therefore," he recalls, "I was most annoyed to have my efforts interrupted by an ironic, down-home voice that struck me as being as irreverent as a honky-tonk trumpet blasting through a performance, say, of Britten's *War Requiem*" (xv). Ellison, who came to New York in 1936 as an aspiring symphonic composer, knows what he is talking about. Nevertheless, as notes from the honky-tonk trumpet invaded his imagination, they challenged him to seize the fire and energy of Invisible Man's jazz voice.

Like Dostoievsky's narrator in *Notes from the Underground*,[3] Invisible Man spoke up uninvited, and unannounced. His was the last voice Ellison wanted to hear. So he jammed Ellison's frequency because it was the only way he could be heard. For although Ellison quickly sensed "that the voice of invisibility issued from deep within our complex American underground," he held back, "still inclined to close my ears and get on with my interrupted novel" (xvii). Ellison tried not to hear because, in his tradition, hearing carries with it a responsibility to respond to what's been said, however marginal the speaker, however discordant and threatening his voice and message. But the jazz voice spoke in an insistent, syncopated rhythm that lured Ellison to imagine "what kind of individual would speak in such accents" (xvii). Consequently, for Ellison as a "fledgling novelist," the problem of voice became the problem of character and form. To *write* a novel, he needed to *hear* this disturbingly familiar voice. And for Invisible Man to exhibit his skill in performance, Ellison needed to create an identity for the "taunting, disembodied voice." "I decided," he writes, "that it would be one who had been forged in the underground of American experience and yet managed to emerge less angry than ironic" (xvii).

Ellison is no longer a resisting or reluctant listener. He becomes a responsive audience and a potentially collaborative author. He openly coaxes Invisible Man to tell the story behind his riff. Soon Ellison sees as well as hears the spokesman for invisibility. He imagines him as "young, powerless (reflecting the difficulties of Negro leaders of the period) and ambitious for a role of leadership; a role at which he was doomed to fail" (xviii) because, among other reasons, he is so slow to grasp what Ellison elsewhere calls "the ambiguity of Negro leadership in the United States" (*SA*, 18).[4] Retrospectively, even as he performs, Ellison distinguishes the task of composition from that of performance. He tells of his effort to tease out the character and story behind the solo voice: "*I* began to structure the movement of my plot while *he* began to merge with my more specialized concerns with fictional form and with certain problems arising out of the pluralistic literary tradition from which I spring" (*IM*, xviii). Slowly, Ellison arrives at a form resilient enough to advance both Invisible Man's distinct, uncategorical voice and identity and the novel's craft.

Ellison is explicit about the new ground he wanted to break with the unsought, unexpected, unwanted, unexpurgated voice of Invisible Man. Meditating on the state of the novel in the 1940s, he wondered "why most protagonists of Afro-American fiction (not to mention the black characters in fiction written by whites) were without intellectual depth" (xviii), which for him was bound up with eloquence and the idea and practice of democracy. "One of the ever present challenges facing the American novelist," he writes, "was that of endowing his inarticulate characters, scenes and social processes with eloquence. For it is by such attempts that he fulfills his social responsibility as an American artist" (xviii).

From his first "taunting, disembodied" utterance, Invisible Man challenges Ellison to write in an urgent vernacular voice and in a form simultaneously novelistic and autobiographical.

Ellison's quest is for eloquence. So is Invisible Man's. Because of the unfinished business of self and American democracy, the act of eloquence is not simple; at times the pursuit of eloquence calls Invisible Man to think while he is acting and, at others, to act while he is thinking. Eloquence is bound up with persuasion, and therefore, Invisible Man's eloquence turns on his ability to improvise in a genuine response to a situation and an actual audience. In a tour de force near the end of his Introduction, Ellison identifies the improvisatory forms and forces urging him to experiment with the novel: "Having worked in barbershops where that form of oral art flourished, I knew that I could draw upon the rich culture of the folk tale as well as that of the novel, and that being uncertain of my skill I would have to improvise upon my materials in the manner of a jazz musician putting a musical theme through a wild starburst of metamorphosis" (xxi). Who in America is not "uncertain of his skill"? And as a test of creative poise and energy, is not improvisation a potential act of eloquence? Ellison's reliance on improvisation reinforces his (and Invisible Man's) theme of identity, and the urgent appearance of an invisible voice in protean form calls for techniques of performance. Furthermore, as a novelist whose sense of improvisatory eloquence is informed by jazz as well as speech, Ellison looks to the jam session for confirmation of his collaboration with Invisible Man.[5]

Ellison's writing on jazz provides a provocative clue to his intentions and highlights the significance of performance in his novel. "In improvised jazz," he said a few years ago, as if to describe *Invisible Man*, "performance and creation can consist of a single complex act."[6] And in a piece on Charlie Christian, Ellison calls jazz a form of combat: "true jazz is an art of individual assertion *within and against* the group" (*SA*, 234; my emphasis). A jazz group achieves its full effect only if the musicians test each others' skills and, through improvisation, explore the full range of each member's untapped potentialities. "Each true jazz moment (as distinct from the uninspired commercial performance) springs from a contest in which each artist challenges all the rest; each solo flight, or improvisation, represents (like the successive canvasses of a painter) a definition of his identity: as individual, as member of the collectivity and as a link in the chain of tradition" (*SA*, 234). Likewise, in the context of the novel, Invisible Man's "taunting, disembodied voice" challenges Ellison to try his skill to the utmost. So too Ellison prods Invisible Man to tell of his efforts to be eloquent simultaneously within and against the grain of his different audiences: black and white, southern and northern, Americans all, optimistic and often confused about the workings of individual and institutional power.

Through his experience as orator and rabble rouser, Invisible Man discovers the combination of luck, will, and skill ("shit, grit, and mother wit") and the coincidence of self and other required in order for "performance and creation" to merge in a "single, complex act." He is so thoroughly a performer that he defines and tests his identity on those occasions when he becomes a public voice. In his speeches, Invisible Man's voice evolves into an instrument more and more keyed to the necessities, limits, and possibilities of call-and-response. To persuade others and move them to action, he relies mostly on techniques of improvisation. Sometimes after the jolt of reversal he learns that his words have consequences dramatically and drastically opposed to his intentions. Several times his speeches lead to unintended actions. For a long time he underestimates the dynamic mutual awareness required between performer and audience for an improvisation to become eloquent. But gradually – too late for a career as an orator, in time for his vocation as a writer – he learns to challenge his audience's skills as well as his own.

Despite his failure to be eloquent with the spoken word, Invisible Man ends up committed to self-reliance as an optimist as well as an ironist. In the novel's paradox, he learns how and why the power of speech can be the power of action only when his potential eloquence falls on closed ears during the chaos of a race riot. In time he comes to see eloquence in much the same way as Ellison's literary ancestor and namesake, Ralph Waldo Emerson, understood it. "There is no orator who is not a hero," Emerson declared. "He is challenged and must answer all comers," and his words evoke Invisible Man's struggle for identity through improvisatory oratory. But the comparison also breaks down because Invisible Man has been too obsessed with advancing "to the top" to embody Emerson's heroic conception of eloquence. "The orator's speech," wrote Emerson in the 1840s when he and others believed in the power of the word to persuade Americans to live out their democratic ideals and free the slaves, "is not to be distinguished from action. *It is the electricity of action.*"[7] Nonetheless, Invisible Man attempts to make Emerson's metaphor work for him. He sends out words like so many charges intended to flow through his audience in a current of action. He misjudges the explosiveness of language and fails as an orator. But later, underground, solitary and silent, he taps into a literal power line and drains off enough electricity from Monopolated Light and Power to provide light and heat while he generates the energy and symbolic action of his autobiography. He tells us this in a voice at once brooding and insulting, peremptory and inquiring, in a Prologue that is the self-conscious "portrait of the artist as rabble-rouser" (*SA*, 179). In his Prologue, Invisible Man does not seek conversation; responsive voices might talk back to him, disagree with him, belittle his point of view, question his motives, undermine his vulnerable, evolving self. Only in the Epilogue, having made ironic peace with his identity and his voice, is he ready for response, for conversation, ready to risk verbal acts of intimacy, ready, in short, for eloquence.

In between, eloquence has a range of Emersonian meanings for Invisible Man. He sets out to be a leader whose speech is action, and not just symbolic action. Later, when he discovers the tricks of false eloquence and the conditions of genuine eloquence, he descends, and aspires, during the interim it takes to write his memoirs, to the symbolic action possible through literary form.[8] His transformation from "an orator, a rabble-rouser," who succeeds or fails, lives or dies through eloquence to a writer learning his craft in underground hibernation involves a reversal of form and identity. As an orator, first freelance and later an employee of the Brotherhood committee, Invisible Man misses the subtle connections between speech and action, performer and audience. In the world, he fails at eloquence and political leadership because he is out of touch, too much an isolated solitary traveler, too much in the grip of illusion (his own and that of others), and because he does not yet understand that he and his words are variables in the American equation of power. Afterward, in the Epilogue, he approaches the question of language and action as a writer able to affirm the very contradictions he resists during his quest for heroic eloquence. Becoming a writer, he transforms the power of the spoken word into the ironic, self-conscious, symbolic potential action of his improvisatory autobiography and Ellison's novel.

2

As he begins to write his story, Invisible Man is suspended between identities. For equilibrium's sake, he clutches his old self: "But I am an orator, a rabble-rouser – Am? I *was,* and perhaps shall be again. Who knows?" (11). Unlike his speeches, which he delivers in the world and presently reconstructs as a writer, his narrative addresses no audience waiting to be moved to particular action on a specific occasion. Nevertheless, he closes the Prologue with a writerly variation on call-and-response. "But what did *I* do to be so blue?" he asks. "Bear with me" (12), he answers, and implies that bearing witness to his tale could make readers participate in a continuing common story. Between the Prologue and the Epilogue, readers enter Invisible Man's mind as he struggles through his speeches, and at other times are present as members of his audiences. As witnesses, we seek to mediate between Invisible Man and his listeners, and so his tale prepares us, too, to take responsibility for our common fate as Americans.

Freedom, an old apparitional slave woman tells Invisible Man, "ain't nothing but knowing how to say what I got up in my head" (9). Often eloquence bursts upon Invisible Man in unexpected, small personal encounters with characters whose living stream of speech feeds the great river of the American language. Such moments of eloquence are affirmations of self, citizenship, and potential national community. But Invisible Man is too absorbed in his career to build a framework of leadership from his encounters with Peter Wheatstraw, Mary Rambo, Tod Clifton, Brother Tarp, and others. Retrospectively, however, he punctuates his passage from orator to writer, innocence to experience and knowledge with a

61

self-conscious, self-critical, and, at the same time, improvisational re-creation of five of his speeches.

The appearance and reality of eloquence coexist uneasily throughout Invisible Man's autobiography. As a young man, his reputation for eloquence rests on an old-fashioned set piece on uplift and humility that he writes, memorizes, and delivers when he graduates from the Negro high school. From his writer's subsequent vantage point, Invisible Man recalls that even then he did not believe that "humility was the secret, indeed, the very essence of progress." "How could I," he asks, "remembering my grandfather? – I only believed that it worked" (14). In his former life, the will to believe returns when he repeats his speech for "the town's leading white citizens." But their agenda is not his. "Told that since I was to be there anyway I might as well take part in the battle royal to be fought by some of my schoolmates as part of the entertainment" (14–15), Invisible Man undergoes initiation into the code of white supremacy in a succession of terrifying, degrading, humiliating rituals. Don't believe any high-faluting praise – especially ours – is the message; your place is the same as that of all other Negroes – at the bottom. As a potential leader of your people, you are especially at the mercy of our money and power. During the battle royal, Invisible Man fights pain and defeat with visions of an oratorical triumph: "I wanted to deliver my speech more than anything else in the world, because I felt that only these men could judge truly my ability" (20). Judge it they do, but the white men judge Invisible Man and the testamental call-and-response form of African-American culture according to the stereotypes of minstrel entertainment.

In his speech, Invisible Man builds his edifice of African-American identity on an old American foundation stone: self-reliant individualism. Naive and ambitious, he does not understand that in this context he cannot answer Emerson's call for the "simple genuine self against the whole world."[9] On the contrary, he inhabits a world of slippery surfaces, sudden depths, and strange forms, a world in which an invisible man needs a trickster's mask, a stance of improvisatory double consciousness if he is to succeed. Half-wittingly, he invokes a tradition. "In those pre-invisible days I visualized myself as a potential Booker T. Washington" (15), and his oration steals its meat from Washington's 1895 Atlanta Exposition Address. But he mistakes an individual or a legend for a tradition. Worse, he has no idea of the contingent relation of language to context, audience, and action. Somehow he cannot imagine that *he*, a young African-American aspiring to racial leadership, would receive a radically different response from "the town's leading white men" than he had from his fellow Negroes. Nor does it occur to him that in their apparent enthusiasm for his praise of humility, the black townspeople may have been putting him on, yessing that naively opportunistic former self of his to death and destruction; or perhaps, like his grandfather, yessing him toward conformity as an ironic tactic of survival.

Although he borrows his words, Invisible Man fails to investigate their rhetorical context. Booker T. Washington possessed more influence than any of the small-town white men Invisible Man addresses at the smoker. That influence was useful and seemingly without menace to whites. In short, Booker T. Washington was somebody, and the leading white citizens of his day knew it. Because of his standing with Negroes and perhaps even more with the northern industrialists and philanthropists the new South needed to advance its economic development, Washington was invited to address the 1895 Exposition. Moreover, there was a certain eloquence about Washington's Address. He rooted the speech in the fallow ground of the Exposition organizers' decision to allow southern Negroes to represent their accomplishments since Emancipation in a separate exhibit. Again and again, Washington based his belief in the mutual progress of the races upon the Exposition; shrewdly, if somewhat self-servingly, he pointed to the invitation issued to him as evidence of social uplift and progress. Though kept separate from one another, both white and Negro citizens were included in the audience. Clearly, Washington's presence and some of his words moved many members of his race to pride, though doubtless some of these same people resented his apparent acquiescence to segregation and to social and political inequality. He pleased white southern and northern establishments because his words came so close to an endorsement of their program. At the same time, near the end of the Address, Washington urged "a determination to administer absolute justice."[10] As a performer, he slipped some strong words into the occasional breaks of his call for accommodation. Washington's oratorical effectiveness stemmed from his painstaking knowledge of American race relations and from his disciplined dedication to what W. E. B. DuBois called the "gospel of Work and Money."[11]

Invisible Man is a nobody, and his reenactment of Washington's words parodies the original occasion. In addition, the smoker's ritual initiation of the next generation into the rules of southern society underlines the failure of Washington's program. "We mean to do right by you," one of the white men tells Invisible Man after his slip of "social equality" for "social responsibility," "but you've got to know your place at all times" (25). The white men mock Invisible Man when he utters a word of "three or more syllables" to teach him that his words are necessarily without power. But about language they are wrong; there is a power in words even on captive occasions. After all, the audience's ridicule releases Invisible Man's deep, long-denied, and unacknowledged thoughts in the charged phrase "social equality." With those two unconsciously intentional words, Invisible Man says *no* to the audience's attempt to make him a mechanical orator and *yes* to the principle of equality affirmed by his grandfather, though seemingly denied; and seemingly affirmed by Jefferson and the other founders, though denied by certain specific provisions the framers built into the Constitution and the American legal code.

In this episode, Invisible Man's set piece is strained to the breaking point by the cruelty of the audience and its abuse of call-and-response. These leading citizens recall Brer Fox and the other animals in the "Tar Baby" tale. Had they let Invisible Man alone, they'd have immobilized the pathetic carcass of his language. Instead, their sadism summons a single eloquent phrase – "social equality" – eloquent because it expresses the capacity of American first principles to emerge in the rhetorical open even on the most degrading occasions. Eloquent too because, for an instant, Invisible Man has publicly avowed and *"yelled* a phrase I had often seen denounced in newspaper editorials, heard debated in private" (24; my emphasis). Doing so, he juxtaposes two traditions: the official white southern written word and the unofficial black southern spoken word.[12] But neither Invisible Man nor his white audience allows his intrusive words to disrupt the social equilibrium. Desperately, each reverts to a corrupt facade of order upheld by ritual. Only briefly do chaos and the possibilities of extemporaneous form unite in the word, and this is due to Invisible Man's subsequent narrative ability to perform with both the written and the spoken word.

3

The state college for Negroes is a training ground for young men aspiring to be leaders of their race. During his time there, Invisible Man encounters several masters of the spoken word. But hearing is not yet thinking for him; he is too mesmerized by words as words to interpret their context. And he does not grasp the nexus between fixed and fluid elements crucial to oral performance. Namely, improvisation is at once incidental and essential to Jim Trueblood's tale and, for that matter, Homer Barbee's Founders' Day sermon; each man delivers an oral set piece embellishing an original story with significant details for the sake of his audience. Trueblood plays the trickster aware that, like the rednecks in the county sheriff's office, the rich white trustee from the North is liable to reward a black sharecropper's tale of incest, properly told. Barbee, the blind black minister, preaches a sermon so spellbinding that his audience, especially the rich white northern trustees, believes that President Bledsoe's ruthless, manipulative, shrewdly masked personal power carries on a mythic past of magic, mystery, and miracle.[13]

In his confrontation with President Bledsoe, Invisible Man continues to downplay the agency of the spoken word. He hears Bledsoe threaten "to have every Negro in the county hanging on tree limbs by morning" (110), and still puts his fate and his faith in words written in a letter he has not seen — a letter he keeps invisible, at Bledsoe's instruction, until it silences him. Up North, unemployed and an outcast, "the more resentful [he] became, the more [his] old urge to make speeches returned" (197). Then, perplexed by an eviction he witnesses on the streets of Harlem, he hears more than he sees:

"Sho, we ought to stop 'em," another man said, "but ain't that much nerve in the whole bunch."

"There's plenty nerve," the slender man said. "All they need is someone to set it off. All they need is a leader. You mean *you* don't have the nerve." (203)

In these spoken words, Invisible Man hears a call for the missing leader. He looks but still does not see until, hearing old Mrs. Provo's voice, he sees that her things reveal his history too, from the *Free Papers* of 1859 to a yellowing newspaper clipping announcing Marcus Garvey's deportation in 1927. In an epiphany, Invisible Man sees the ancestral past littered on the street. He witnesses the refusal of Mrs. Provo's request to go inside for a last prayer. In response, the crowd sways toward action — "To hell with all this talk, let's rush the bastard." Invisible Man experiences a rush of ambivalent energy, for the very renunciation of language affirms the power of the word. "I was both afraid and angry, repelled and fascinated. I both wanted it and feared the consequences, was outraged and angered at what I saw and yet surged with fear" (208) at the chaos and danger of violence. Instead, he pursues symbolic, verbal action. Instinctively, he pushes his way forward, "talking rapidly without thought but out of my clashing emotions" (209), as if the act of speech would give coherence to his thoughts.

As public discourse, Invisible Man's eviction speech seems an absurdity, for it affirms the reverse of what is happening. In it he improvises *against* the crowd's potential for action. He begins saying *no* to the crowd by saying *yes*. "We're a law-abiding people and a slow-to-anger people," he calls out. Perhaps because his words contradict the people's mood, his speech has briefly the effect he desires. "They stopped, listening. Even the white man was stilled" (209). But the performance stalls because Invisible Man proposes no alternative action to the angry crowd, and this failure of improvisation marks the limits of his eloquence. Because his initial gesture possesses some of the electricity of action, his speech produces an effect antithetical to his intention. Once again he fails to intuit or analyze his context, fails to grasp that his audience resents its reputation as a law-abiding, slow-to-anger group. Therefore an ironic collaboration occurs between Invisible

66

Man and his audience. Accommodate, he urges, perhaps again echoing Booker T. Washington's southern strategy, but his words remind these northern Negroes of why they came North, remind them of injustice too long passively endured. They interrupt his speech not to encourage him, as members of a congregation might, but to silence him because his speech threatens to rob them of bold action. In effect, Invisible Man and his audience reverse call-and-response. Although he fears their point of view, he adapts and changes his pitch. He must, if he wishes to keep on talking – and words are essential to a leader's identity.

For instance, trying to make a case for a southern Negro school principal who turned over a fugitive to "the forces of law and order," he yields the point when a woman angrily contradicts him:

> "He was a handkerchief-headed rat!" a woman screamed, her voice boiling with contempt.
> "Yes, you're right. He was wise and cowardly, but what about us? What are we to do?" I yelled, suddenly thrilled by the response. "Look at him" I cried.
> "Yes, just look at him!" an old fellow in a derby called out as though answering a preacher in church. (209–10)

Even though the woman's response derides his anecdote and his point of view, he performs two quick modulations that exhibit his native gifts. He agrees with the antagonistic woman, softens and complicates her violent rhetoric, then abruptly refocuses on old Primus Provo's predicament. His recall of Provo summons an affirmative response, and Invisible Man resumes his earlier attempt to tell the story of African-American history by breathing significance into the inanimate personal effects and household possessions strewn along the curb. For a time, his words rechannel the people's energy into reflection as he seeks a middle ground between caution and recklessness. But he finds none, and instead plays off the audience's belligerent response to his stalling: " 'Dispossessed?' That's a good word, 'Dispossessed.' " But he has no nonviolent option left except to challenge the marshall: "How about it, Mr. Law? Do we get our fifteen minutes worth of Jesus?' " (211).

Invisible man fails to hold the moment in suspension for two reasons: first, because those carrying out the eviction order are closed to possibility, and, second, because the crowd has in mind a preconceived response to the situation. "Where do we go?" he asks, and first one, then another, and another answer by rushing past him. Throughout his speech, they've been ready to overpower the cops and repossess the apartment. Finally, aroused by his words, they overcome the restraint implicit in his rhetorical question. Intriguingly, Invisible Man doesn't sulk. He doesn't run off. He lends his voice to their action: " 'We're dispossessed,' " I sang at the top of my voice, 'dispossessed and we want to pray. Let's go in and pray. Let's have a big prayer meeting. But we'll need some chairs to sit in. . . . rest upon as we kneel. We'll need some chairs!' " (213). Invisible Man's rhythm and repetition transcend the literal meaning of his words. He stays because these people have been a participatory audience and because he has become implicated in their action. By improvising he participates, "no longer struggling against or thinking about the nature of my action" (213). At every point, he follows the lead of his audience. He wanted to calm them and assert his right to leadership; instead, he stirs them up and they literally push him out of the way. Again, the power of words is not static, stable, or containable; when spoken, words can lead to contingent, unanticipated, unsought consequences different from the speaker's intention and his version of their meaning. In love with the idea of eloquence, Invisible Man follows the people in a response explicitly denied but implicitly affirmed by his words.

At a submerged level, Invisible Man understands his essentially passive role in the people's action. Others, however, do not. Brother Jack, a witness to the performance, recruits Invisible Man for the Brotherhood organization because he has use for the young man's vagrant, unfocused, uncontextualized capacity for eloquence. But he misunderstands what has happened. "You aroused them so quickly to action," he tells Invisible Man. "With a few words you had them involved in action" (219). Jack's explanation misreads the complex, contingent relationship between audience and performer. Because of his collectivist, scientific ideology, he refuses to recognize that a personal, emotional bond galvanizes Invisible Man and the other black individuals into a sense of community. To Jack, Invisible Man is nothing more or

68

less than a black *voice* worthy only to serve the Brotherhood's program. "You shall be the new Booker T. Washington, but even greater than he" (233), he tells Invisible Man, defining him historically before he writes down a new name for him. For his part, Invisible Man resolves to have "one of us, in at the beginning of something big"; and besides, he thinks, "if I refused to join them where would I go — to a job as porter at the railroad station? *At least here was a chance to speak*" (234; my emphasis). As elsewhere, he defines his freedom and ambition in terms of public speaking but leaves others to define language, leadership, and power.

4

When Invisible Man makes his first speech for the Brotherhood, he believes his words capable of fusing his interests with those of his race and the organization.[14] Approaching the microphone, he sees as one audience the Brotherhood committee on the stage and the crowd sitting in the Harlem arena. The unfamiliar microphone enables him to forge a bond with his audience and to generate the theme of his speech. "It looks like the steel skull of a man! Do you think he died of dispossession?" (250). In the best improvisatory tradition, he makes the microphone a complementary, almost totemic, instrument, and so turns a potentially disabling mechanical difficulty into an occasion for contact. The response from the audience — "We with you, Brother. You pitch 'em we catch em!" — confirms his sense of power with words and kinship with those who listen to him. "That was all I needed," he remembers; "I'd made a contact, and it was as though his voice was that of them all" (258). In a widening circle of reciprocity, speaker and listener testify for each other, and together they speak for the entire audience.

Currents of energy now flow toward Invisible Man. Charged, he looks to the audience as a congregation, a community with shared values and objectives. The people's responses compensate for his feeble command of Brotherhood literature. "I couldn't remember the correct words and phrases from the pamphlets," but the voice from the crowd, like the evicted couple's possessions, connects him with his past. "I had to fall back upon tradition and since it was a political meeting, I selected one of the political techniques that I'd heard so often at home: The old, down-to-earth, I'm sick-and-tired-of-the-way-they've-been-treating-us approach" (258–9). He recognizes eloquence as his sole coin, but eloquence without any particular ideology or program. Here, as so often happens in the novel, Invisible Man draws on both American and African-American traditions. No doubt, he has heard the populist oratory of white southern politicians, a few of whom appealed to the black poor even during the decades of disenfranchisement. But Invisible Man also borrows from "the Negro church, wherein," Ellison recalls in "Remembering Richard Wright," "you heard the lingering accents of 19th century rhetoric with its emphasis upon freedom and individual responsibility; a rhetorical style which gave us Lincoln, Harriet Tubman, Harriet Beecher Stowe and other abolition-preaching Beechers. Which gave us Frederick Douglass and John Jasper and many other eloquent and heroic Negroes whose spirit still moves among us through the contributions which they made to the flexibility, the music and idealism of the American language."[15] Thematically too, the speech's trajectory moves from politics to personality, with dispossession the bridge between two imperatives: identity and equality.

Throughout, Invisible Man employs call-and-response. He testifies to his and his audience's complicity in their dispossession through images and metaphors of vision. Soon, however, he exhausts the political theme and, in the midst of applause, "realized that the flow of words had stopped" (260–1). So far, he's been using his voice to summon a vision suitable for almost any group, any occasion, and perfectly compatible, he thinks, with this rally and its mixed audience. Now though, emptied of the familiar, he must improvise a new story to go with the devices of the oral tradition. But how, since he has no program of action, no promise of revolution, no specific vision of a different society? All he has is an existence verified by the response of the audience. Therefore, Invisible Man modulates from a vague political rhetoric into a confessional voice. His emerging "more human" identity, he tells them, awaits their confirmation.

Oratory yields to storytelling. Encouraged by another response in the form of a gentle personal question, he comes home rhetorically and declares himself "a new citizen of the country of your vision" (262). But the listeners' vision flows from his words, and the speech's formulaic ending transforms dispossession into a spontaneous, briefly powerful kinship, incipiently political and perhaps racial, as well as strongly personal. Call-and-response turns I and you into we as Invisible Man names his audience the "PATRIOTS AND CITIZENS OF TOMORROW'S WORLD" (262). He strains eloquence to the limit, puts his identity on the line. and persuasively, safely, vaguely asserts the potentiality of action. But he does so outside the Brotherhood's scientific framework and political program. He generates the preliminary electricity of action by virtue of his sudden authority as an articulate presence and personality able to perform so that he and his audience, for an instant, become one.

Afterward, Invisible Man learns that his speech and technique displease most of the Brotherhood committee. Brother Jack approves because he thinks the people have coalesced and are therefore "just waiting to be told what to do" (263). But the pure ideologues resist Jack's non sequitur and accuse Invisible Man of a "wild, hysterical, politically irresponsible and dangerous" speech antithetical to the Brotherhood's ideology. Both miss the point, though the critics have the better of the argument. The audience was moved because of Invisible Man's creation of an identity in response to its participatory voices. Although that moment passes, any action in the future also depends on participation, because, as the ideologues recognize better than Jack, the contact point between Invisible Man and the audience has been defiance of externally imposed authority.

In a self-conscious meditation later that night, Invisible Man assesses what happened to him during the speech. The person who emerged and the voice that spoke strike him as strangers, intruders – perhaps in the way Ellison formerly considered Invisible Man's "taunting, disembodied voice" an act of intrusion. "What had come out was completely uncalculated, as though another self within me had taken over and held forth." He finds his technique radically changed; "no one who had known me at college would have recognized the speech" (267). Later, when Invisible Man takes his cue from confidence man B. P. Rinehart,

71

identity changes according to disguises of dress and appearance; here, self corresponds to the guises of speech. "I *was* someone new," he muses, struck by the paradox, "even though I had spoken in a very old-fashioned way" (267). Until the eviction speech and his performance in the arena, Invisible Man identifies eloquence with oratorical set pieces whose formalized delivery is intended to shut the gates of the self – for both speaker and audience – against terrors of the unexpected, the taboo. What he calls "very old-fashioned" approaches the testamental, participatory, rejuvenating forms of the oral tradition, the contemporary improvisations of jazz as well as the rhetoric of southern politicians and preachers. For eloquence depends on the speaker's expression of what is happening at the moment of performance – the ability to reveal his identity as it develops in response to the immediate audience and perhaps a larger implicit audience attuned to similar experience and traditions.

In this sense, Invisible Man's newness emerges from his interplay with his audience. When he spoke of what was happening to him, he shed some of the old limits of self and story, because he was not supposed to reveal his story. His identification, if not his identity, is newly invented, his new name written down by the Brotherhood, and his story is supposed to unfold under official conditions as controlled as those of a scientific experiment. But without verbal kinship with his audience, an improvisatory speaker loses the power of speech. "They had wanted me to succeed, and fortunately I had spoken for them and they had recognized my words. I belonged to them" (267). Invisible Man's conclusion signals the dangerous contingency of improvisation – a speaker's temptation to derive his identity from his audience. In the way he has done with individuals, Invisible Man embraces the audience's power to define his actions. "The audience was mixed, their claims broader than race. I would do whatever was necessary to serve them well." And he acknowledges a frightening prospect: "How else could I save myself from disintegration?" (267). Apparently, now, his coherence as a human being depends on service and on confirmation by those served.

Paradoxically, his analysis inclines him to hand others the right to judge his performance. He does not question or test his premise that he has "become more human" by virtue of his call-and-response improvisation with the audience. Instead, he affirms the mystery of words but, characteristically, subordinates the mystery to his personal agenda of ambition and success. "Here was a way to have a part in making the big decisions, of seeing through the mystery of how the country, the world, really operated. . . . I had only to work and learn and survive in order to go to the top" (268). The top is not the mountain top; he wants to make it in American society and, like Bledsoe, will use others, black and white, to climb the mountain. At this point, both eloquence and the country (the word and the world) are mysteries Invisible Man regards as keys to power. The pursuit of power is a secret kept uneasily by Invisible Man, since he has yet to build a bridge of words and action between self and American democratic ideals. Equally important, he has yet to penetrate the ambiguities of the pursuit of an African-American political agenda and the theory and practice, the power relationships, of American politics. Unlike Booker T. Washington, the historical archetype of this section of the novel, Invisible Man finds a constituency but lacks a political program. Unlike the cautious and prepared Washington, who always knew who he was, for Invisible Man eloquence has become solely the art of improvisation. He forgets the counsel of his former literature teacher: "Our task is that of making ourselves individuals" (268). Obsessed with making *it*, he resists the knowledge that his cultural identity and his words need to become more than nervous reflexes if he is to find his way through the labyrinth of American society.

5

After Invisible Man becomes the chief spokesman of the Harlem District, Brother Tarp gives him a portrait of Frederick Douglass. Douglass "belongs to all of us," Tarp tells him, and Douglass replaces Booker T. Washington as the ancestral model of African-American eloquence and leadership. As a leader, Invisible Man rallies the community behind the Brotherhood agenda. Soon he feels his "old self" slipping out of touch with "the new public self that spoke for the Brotherhood" (287), but he responds to this danger by rekindling his urge to personal power. The Brotherhood "was the one organization in the whole country in which I could reach the very top and I meant to get there" (286, 287).[16] He vows to climb "a mountain of words" and confesses his belief that "there was a magic in spoken words." He focuses on Douglass, not as Tarp has done, as a leader of and for the people, but as an archetype of individual success – a fellow orator who "had talked his way from slavery to a government ministry" (288). He notes that Douglass too had "taken another name" but does not mention Douglass's eloquence as a writer or his ability to use autobiographical narratives to complement the rhetoric of his speeches.[17]

Preoccupied with personal destiny, Invisible Man forgets that Douglass's power was bound up with the personal, racial, national cause of freedom and justice. Besides, Douglass used the force of his words and personality to change the thinking of powerful individuals and organizations. He persuaded others to his articulate vision and moved them to action, whereas Invisible Man seems to encourage the Brotherhood to manipulate him. For instance, accused of having a personality cult, he is suspended from his leadership position in Harlem and sent "to lecture downtown on the Woman Question." In an arrogant parting shot, Brother Jack tells him, "My pamphlet, 'On the Woman Question in the United States' will be your guide" (306, 307). Invisible Man's assignment stirs memories of Douglass speaking for women's rights. Without his eloquent speech to the 1848 Seneca Falls Convention, the resolution endorsing votes for women would almost certainly have failed, and he spoke to a women's rights group in Washington, D.C., on the day he died. Douglass did none of these things – or little else in his life – as a consequence of someone's orders. Like Abraham Lincoln, who was both ally and adversary, colleague and equal in the struggle for democracy, he lived out Emerson's imperative that the orator be a general whose "speech must be just ahead of the assembly, ahead of the whole human race, or it is superfluous."[18] But Invisible Man ignores Douglass's fraternal example and leaves Harlem without a word of explanation or farewell to Brother Clifton, Brother Tarp, or anyone else who has helped him.

Summoned back to Harlem by the committee months later, he

finds Clifton vanished and the Brotherhood operation nearly defunct. "There had had been, to my surprise," he notes in the bloodless, euphemistic language of the party line, "a switch in emphasis from local issues to those more national and international in scope, and it was felt that for the moment the interests of Harlem were not of first importance" (324). He fails to interpret Clifton's departure as a response to the Brotherhood's betrayal of political principle and his (Invisible Man's) betrayal of fraternal principle. Only when he happens on Clifton performing an ironic minstrel show with papier-mâché Sambo dolls does Invisible Man realize that others see him as the Brotherhood's ventriloquist's dummy – "he'll kill your depression and your dispossession" (327). Humiliated into inarticulate fury, Invisible Man watches in silence as Clifton is gunned down by a white policeman. Back in Harlem, denied access to the Brotherhood committee, Invisible Man acts from "personal responsibility" and organizes a public funeral.

As he looks down from the speaker's platform, amazed at the enormous turnout, he asks two silent, related questions. "Did it signify love or politicized hate? And could politics ever be an expression of love?" (341). Rooted in his own muddled motives, his questions nevertheless reach out toward that American and African-American conviction that an individual's deepest personal beliefs and experience are somehow bound up with the political life of the nation. When he looks out and sees faces in the crowd, Invisible Man realizes that for these people politics is an expression of love in the complex sense identified by Ellison as "that condition of man's being at home in the world which is called love and which we term democracy" (*SA*, 106). In this context, Invisible Man seeks fraternity and community, if not democracy. Unexpectedly, he hears the sudden solo voice of an old man raised in "Many a Thousand Gone" and suddenly understands that for these people love intensifies the engagement with the world that becomes inevitably political. To this man and those who hear him in the burning heat, Tod Clifton is more than an individual. He was an individual man, yes, and to be praised for his step, his quick hands, his love for his people expressed in his style as much as in his politics. But now he has become one of the many thousands gone, the victims of racial injustice. And so they mourn him doubly in the testamental tradition. The "old plaintive, masculine voice" of the singer, "stumbling in the silence at first alone," is answered by someone on a euphonium horn. The painful, lovely duet leads more and more people in a collective improvisatory expression of grief, struggle, and transformation.

Invisible Man muses enviously on the old man's power to move the people and his own apparent lack of eloquence. "It was as though," he reflects, "the song had been there all the time and he knew it and aroused it; and I knew that I had known it too and had failed to release it out of a vague, nameless shame or fear. But he had known it and aroused it" (342). This man has no narrow political or personal stake in the funeral. His act of voice becomes a citizen's fraternal call answered in kind by the crowd. Whatever the past defeats and continuing obstacles, he and they aspire to be at home in the world. And at last, Invisible Man shares the kinship, aware that the song goes on within him too and that its words and performance "had touched something deeper than protest or religion" (342).

Invisible Man feels "deepened by that *something* for which the theory of Brotherhood had given me no name" (342; my emphasis). His *something* is deliberately, necessarily vague, expressively so; perhaps, like the *somehow* in Lincoln's second Inaugural Address, the word assumes palpability in this context. "All knew," Lincoln said as the Civil War was ending, "that this interest was somehow, the cause of the war." Lincoln bore witness to his and his fellow citizens' consciousness that underneath the arguments and statistics, the explanations and rationalizations, underneath logic and language too, the question of slavery and the fate of the African-American provided an uncategorical, irreducible, decisive, and in some sense mysterious test for democracy. Language and action expressed equally a private and public commitment to love and politics. Likewise, in Harlem's Mount Morris Park, Invisible Man and all who hear the song are moved by feelings deeper than that "old longing, resigned, transcendent emotion" summoned by "the same old slave-borne words" (342). The rendition of "Many a Thousand Gone" arises from present circumstance and past experience. The song joins the people as listeners and participants who know that in the midst of life and death the struggle for freedom goes on. It continues through expressions of personality that lead people to stop, to think and feel, and see the end and the beginning of things in the life around them. Some tangle of kindred thought and emotion, some new responsiveness, leads Invisible Man to accept grudgingly, if not to affirm, the place of inarticulateness, the word groped for, felt but not yet found, the word as sign of the speaker's inability to penetrate and solve the mysteries of experience.

Strangely, Invisible Man's inarticulate response flows from the tones of the song. "I had no words," he remembers, and when he does speak, his words sound harsh, as if resisting the need to respond to the call of the song. " 'What are you waiting for me to tell you?' I shouted," and he follows with a bitter riff that leads into his ironic refrain: "Go home." But he doesn't fool the people; they know from his tone that something else is happening. And they listen to his denial of eloquence in an appropriate way. "They were listening intently, and as though looking not at me, but at the pattern of my voice upon the air" (343). What matters more than his words is the rising and falling, fluid pattern of his voice – his articulate/inarticulate struggle to form connections between his identity and theirs. "Go home," he repeats over and over, but, really, they are home at this moment in their park. Still, "they gave no sign," so he tells them the story of Clifton's life and death – his murder. As he speaks, he feels desperately empty and inarticulate, almost nauseous over his unwitting but terribly consequential betrayal of Clifton and his audience, the people of Harlem. "It wasn't political," he thinks, but he is wrong. He does not know it, but his speech improvises on the song, theirs and his. It answers the question about politics and love in concrete terms, public and private, biographical and autobiographical. Clifton's work flowed from love, and so does the people's presence. Invisible Man's speech, shouted with no microphone for support, becomes political exactly because he sees Clifton now as someone he could not formerly love because of his narrow ambitions.

His words re-create Clifton as part of the community's inner and outer life, someone who, if he could speak, would utter words fusing love and politics. "Tell them," he says, using Clifton's rhythm and style, "to get out of the box and to teach the cops to forget that rhyme. Tell them to teach them that when they call you *nigger* to make a rhyme with *trigger* it makes the gun backfire" (346). Yet Invisible Man curiously exhorts his audience to fold up its tent and "go home, keep cool, stay safe away from the sun" (346): the last things they will do. Once again, the effect of Invisible Man's words differs from what he thinks he's produced. "I stood looking at the crowd with a sense of failure. I had let it get away from me, had been unable to bring in the political issues" (356). His mind's logic lags behind the actual energy of his words. Granted, he does not leave the people in a fighting mood according to the precepts of classical oratory. Better, for his political purposes, he leaves them with smoldering thoughts of how closely they (and he) are bound up with Clifton's "plunge outside of history" (331). Something is going on, moved by Invisible Man's speech, in which he merges the rhetoric and technique of a preacher with those of a savvy contemporary storyteller. Silenced by his own on-again-off-again performance, Invisible Man for the first time sees an audience in its own reality, distinct from his identity, his agenda. Most importantly, "as I took one last look I saw not a crowd, but the set faces of individual men and women" (347). Somewhere in a corner of his mind, he realizes that the people may be temporarily in hibernation, a point he does not reach until the narrative's events are over, a state of being he then defines as "a covert preparation for a more overt action" (11). The words of the old song and his improvised speech move the people to a determined, anticipatory silence. Though understood, the lesson remains unspoken: To have "social responsibility," you've got to be willing and able to take "personal responsibility," just as earlier it is implied that true "social responsibility" flows from the condition of "social equality." To become a community, individual men and women must be "capable of their own action" (414).

6

As he writes, Invisible Man's vision of the crowd as individuals turns into an important revelation, but immediately after the funeral he does not grasp the reversal that once again makes him follow the lead of the people. He creeps along, "confused and listless moving through crowds that seemed to boil along in a kind of mist." Resisting the crowd's palpable and impalpable fluidity, Invisible Man fusses: "plans had to be made; the crowd's emotion had to be organized" (347). Meanwhile, the Brotherhood committee is furious at his twin improvisations of funeral and speech. In a meeting, Brother Jack mocks Invisible Man's explanatory words – "on your personal re-spon-si-bility." His parody of call-and-response recalls the smoker where the white men demand jeeringly that Invisible Man repeat the phrase "social responsibility." Jack's categories deny the transforming energy that flows between speaker and audience during an improvisation. His ideology divides consciousness from language, language from action, and denies an orator full access to those he nourishes and is nourished by.

In a passionate response to Jack's accusations, Invisible Man affirms the complexity and autonomy of his people. "The Brotherhood isn't the Negro people; no organization is" (353). Consequently, he testifies to (and embodies) a context wherein his mind and the people's are activated and revealed by their voices. "Listen some Saturday damn near anywhere in Harlem," he tells them – "A whole unrecorded history is spoken there, Brother" – and then he advances toward an American vernacular destination. Experience, Emerson's companion to eloquence, is the territory Invisible Man lights out for: "I stand on what I see and feel and on what I've heard, and what I know" (356). Nonetheless, Invisible Man continues to affirm his Brotherhood life on the ground that, despite its hypocrisies and outrages, "it was the only historically meaningful life that I could live" (361). Only when his private tutor reveals the secret party line does Invisible Man become, after his grandfather's example, "a traitor" and "a spy in the enemy's country" (13). "It's impossible *not* to take advantage of the people," Brother Hambro informs him. "The trick is to take advantage of them in their own best interest" (381). Hearing this Bledsonian cynicism, Invisible Man, alone and stunned, reels into the street: First in reverie and later in the act of writing, he becomes able "to articulate the issues which tortured [him]" (xviii). Because he is still unaware that the people's capacity to speak an eloquent "un-recorded history" implies a capacity for action, Invisible Man seeks some "firm ground for action that would lead them onto the plane of history." But the people have been standing their ground on the *plains* of history longer than he knows, and how *absurd*, to use one of his favorite words, is the idea that he "would have to move them without [himself] being moved" (383).

Certainly, he slips and slides while seeking a foothold on his "mountain of words." To find one, he seizes on a new-found ability "to look around corners" and accept all of his "separate experiences," no matter how foolish or bizarre. "They were me; they defined me. I was my experiences and my experiences were me, and no blind men, no matter how powerful they became, even if they conquered the world, could take that, or change one single itch, taunt, laugh, cry, scar, ache, rage or pain of it" (383). This eloquent riff becomes public only when he writes it down later and it is read. Yet in its private form it prepares him for his climactic encounter with the world, a reality he now acknowledges as more important than Brotherhood and other narrow categories of perception and experience.

Suddenly but inevitably, those "set faces of individual men and women" who had listened silently to his funeral speech a few days before release their anger and passion in wild, riotous actions, some individual, some collective. Rushing uptown, Invisible Man experiences an old reflex to *lead* somehow, but once in Harlem he is happy to melt into the occasion. Hit by a bullet, he is stunned into "a sudden and brilliant [and dangerous] suspension of time" (404) before he is rescued by some men he's never seen before (or even imagined). They seize the chance to burn down the tenement in which they've lived their unnoticed lives. For Invisible Man, this action and the manner of its execution stand as the most revealing political and personal experience in the novel. As Dupre, Scofield, and others prepare their work, Invisible Man is struck by Dupre's simple, direct, spontaneous exercise of leadership. "And let's have some organization," he says, in words that parody the Brotherhood's posturing about leaders and the people and demonstrate how effective leadership emerges from a particular context.

The egos of Scofield and his companions become one with the flow of the action.

Caught in this rhythm, Invisible Man carries a bucket of coal oil. Characteristically, he broods: "What was the meaning of it all? What should I think of it, do about it?" (410). But his observer's pose dissolves into a participatory response to the moment. "And now," he remembers as he relives the experience, "I was seized with a sense of exultation. They've done it, I thought. They organized it and carried it through alone; the decision their own and their own action. Capable of their own action" (414). He is illuminated and transformed. Retrieving his briefcase from one of the tenement landings, he grabs a bucket of kerosene and hurls it into a burning room. For the first time, he expresses his urge toward eloquence in action, not words, and becomes the deed.

Almost immediately, another chance experience reforms his personality and rejuvenates him. Words are the catalyst, this time spoken by individuals he does not know, people whose lives he's held of little account. He overhears a man tell a woman, "If it become a sho' nough race riot I want to be here where there'll be some fighting back." With terrific, unexpected force, "the words struck like bullets fired close range, blasting my satisfaction to earth." Another crazy reversal occurs on this night of chaos, for words overpower Invisible Man's consciousness as the real bullet failed to do to his flesh. "It was as though the uttered word had given meaning to the night, almost as though it had created it" (417), he remembers, and now, as then, the word arouses his mind and imagination. When the man's words explode "against the loud, riotous air," Invisible Man constructs an interpretation of the events he's been witnessing and experiencing. To fight without guns is suicide, he thinks, and as the scale of the Brotherhood's manipulation, machination, and complicity sinks in, he imagines the outcome as mass murder, perhaps planned by the committee.

At length, he has the climactic encounter of the night and the narrative – a final contest with his nemesis, Ras the Exhorter, now Ras the Destroyer, as that rabble-rouser's leadership also turns from words to deeds. Coincidentally yet predictably and implacably, Invisible Man crosses the path of Ras's inflamed band of black nationalist followers. His sunglasses broken and therefore his Rinehart disguise shattered, he dicovers new meaning and potentiality in the signs of previous experience. Brother Tarp's leg chain becomes brass knuckles and the locked and laden briefcase a club, but most of all, Invisible Man acts with a calm sureness that comes from "a new sense of self." Reflexes of consciousness, language, and action flow as one: "I knew suddenly what I had to do, knew it even before it shaped itself completely in my mind" (420). Yet first, he sticks to his habit of trying to be effective with articulate, improvisational words in the form of a speech.

If the context were different, his uttered words might be eloquent, that is, persuasive and consequential. In a dramatic reversal, he implicates the Brotherhood in a scheme to manipulate blacks to participate in the developing race riot for the organization's propaganda advantage. But Invisible Man's interpretation and exhortation are contrary to Ras's lust for violence, his determination to use the riot for his own ends. "Grab him," Ras commands, and instinctively, "without thinking," Invisible Man fuses a word — "No" — with "a desperate oratorical gesture of disagreement and defiance." He wrenches Ras's spear free, "gripping it mid-shaft, point forward," and spells out simply and powerfully the meaning behind the chaos of this crazy night:

> "They want this to happen," I said. "They planned it. They want the mobs to come uptown with machine guns and rifles. They want the streets to flow with blood; your blood, black blood and white blood, so that they can turn your death and sorrow and defeat into propaganda. It's simple, you've known it a long time. It goes, 'Use a nigger to catch a nigger.' Well, they used it to catch you and now they're using Ras to do away with me and to prepare your sacrifice. Don't you see it? Isn't it clear . . . ?" (421)

Invisible Man's use of call-and-response is contingent, and the effect varies according to the different contexts of his spoken and written words. Now, in the continuing present of his narrative act, the words form an eloquent truth that reverberates in the world. But on that chaotic night in the past, his words inspire only Ras's call for a murderous act. " 'Hang the lying traitor,' Ras shouted. 'What are you waiting for' " (421). "Wait," Invisible Man cries and stops, as if struck dumb. For the first time, he feels and understands the contingencies of language and the limits of eloquence. "I had no words and no eloquence" (422), he thinks then, and in the narrative present writes how he performed the negating and affirming act of ceasing to speak. On the page, the words he has spoken are direct, stunning, and convincing, but as spoken words they lack transforming power because no bond of consciousness exists any longer with his audience. Performance and creation, improvisation and eloquence – leadership, he recognizes at last – depend on readiness, responsiveness, and fluidity by both speaker and audience. If either becomes antagonistic, there can be no true call-and-response; without the possibility of love, there is only the politics of hate.

Then and now, his words backfire. But they also reverberate in a self-revelation experienced that night and made eloquently, forcefully articulate during the time he performs (and Ellison composes) the narrative. He is and was, he realizes, "no hero, but short and dark with only a certain eloquence and a bottomless capacity for being a fool to mark me from the rest." *Hearing* who he is, he sees his audience too: "saw them, recognized them at last as those whom I had failed and of whom I was not, just now, a leader, though leading them, running ahead of them, only in the stripping away of my illusionment" (422). As Ellison thirty years later tells us would be the case with such an underground African-American *character*, Invisible Man at the moment of self-recognition affirms the momentary, reverse English quality of his leadership in a voice audibly "less angry than ironic" (xvii). In an exemplary verbal act, he peels the disguising, distorting illusion from the edifice of his personality. But his audience does not follow. And why should it on an instant's notice, since in the past he has put eloquence in the service of illusions – his, his listeners', and worse, his (and their) manipulators'?

Now, for an unbearably, necessarily long instant between his last spoken word and his violent preemptive gesture, Invisible Man looks at death and listens to its voice. Would death at the hands of his listeners instruct them about their true identity? Yes, he decides stoically, it might "perhaps move them one fraction of a bloody step closer to a definition of who they were and of what I was and had been." "But," he goes on in a swerving reversal, "the definition would have been too narrow." He is right: "it was better to live out one's own absurdity than to die for that of others, whether for Ras's or Jack's" (422). Besides, from his interior monologue radiate words that resonate with the riddle of nationhood and the paradox of individual citizenship. "The beautiful absurdity of their American identity and mine" is the text, and these words might well be the novel's epigraph. But at the time of this experience, eloquence fails because there is no way for Invisible Man to break the pattern of conflict.

"A cry on the perilous edge of the fight," Emerson demanded from any orator who aspired to eloquence, "or let him be silent."[19] Aided by his meditation, Invisible Man conjures silence into action. He improvises a violent, eloquent gesture. He throws the spear back at Ras, and unlike his words, the weapon finds its mark. It penetrates Ras's cheeks and locks his jaws, silencing him. But as he flees, Invisible Man pines after the healing power of the spoken word. He wishes he could lay down his improvised weapons of briefcase and leg iron and say to his pursuers: "Look men, give me a break, we're all black folks together" (423). But it's no good, and he knows it. Invisible Man cannot successfully invoke the theme of African-American solidarity with Ras's men. How can he when just now he has made their leader another of the "many a thousand gone"? For the moment, Invisible Man will have to be satisfied with "silence, exile, and cunning"[20] – the weapons of Joyce's Stephen Dedalus, another man destined to be his own father – if he is to have a chance to pursue eloquence underground in the form and voice of the written word.

"The beautiful absurdity of [our] American identity": Invisible Man hears his proposition enacted as soon as he eludes Ras's gang and before he descends into a manhole to avoid a pair of murderous whites. Then he overhears two black men describe Ras's antics. They do not see him in black nationalist or African tribal terms. Instead, they identify him with vernacular American culture, with that archetypal white cowboy hero, the Lone Ranger: for good measure, one of the men riffs that Ras's *black* " 'hoss shot up the street like Heigho, the goddamn Silver' " (426). Because two black men he's never seen before discover an American identity common to both Ras and the Lone Ranger, Invisible Man changes his mind, as he's had to do so many times after chance encounters with eloquent, unknown African-Americans. Indignant, he nevertheless allows this perspective, which *he* never could have imagined, to penetrate his mind. Yes, Ras's performance is as *funny* as these street characters suggest in their rich, irreverent, defiant vernacular. It's also dangerous, as Invisible Man realizes before he puts a violent end to that performance. And if there is tragedy here, it does not undermine Invisible Man's will to meet life in its mad, endlessly various guises and disguises. In the midst of everything – pain and loss, love and hate, politics and propaganda – the rich act of vernacular speech urges Invisible Man to challenge what Ellison calls the "apparent forms of reality" (*SA*, 114).

7

It remains for Invisible Man to replace the "apparent forms of reality" with a visible form of his own. He realizes that he "had been used as a tool" (426), and that in his case the tool was the spoken word. Rightly, he now fears dispossession of voice. In his underground nightmare at the close of the narrative proper, he dreams that Jack and other adversaries castrate him and hang his testicles "*beneath the apex of the curving arch of the bridge*" overhead (430). His sexual parts stand for all of those illusions that have nourished his false identities. The nightmare ends when "the bridge seemed to move off to where I could not see, striding like a robot, an iron man, whose iron legs clanged doomfully as it moved." Invisible Man's illusions crank the bridge into an enormous robot endowed with motion and an insensate, terrifying quasi-voice. "*No, no, we must stop him'*" (431), he shouts to no one and then awakens to the desolate silence of his underground dwelling.

In the Epilogue, Invisible Man puzzles out the terms of his nightmare. How can he say "we," for instance? Alone and underground, cut off from responsive human contact, how can he warn against his apparition of conformity's totalitarian technological soul? In an improvisational response to the story he has just written down, he tries to tell what is happening now that he has changed his vocation from orator to writer, especially "what was happening when your eyes were looking through" (439). His performance as a writer testifies to his past failure as a rabble rouser, a leader, and a speaker. But even as he meditates on failures of eloquence with the spoken word, he achieves eloquence as a writer by relying on an urgent but unintimidating conversational style. The Epilogue is not merely meditation; in it Invisible Man forges a style by responding to what he imagines are his readers' (listeners' too, imaginatively) observations on his and his country's evolving identity. He intends all of this as an example to his readers. They (really we), if moved and persuaded by his views of selfhood and nationhood, are free to improvise a response. We may, in diverse ways, combine creation and performance in many individual complex acts that follow from his author's act of leadership. These are some of the possibilities he articulates when he suggests in his last words, and asks us to confirm, that he speaks for us.

Invisible Man complicates the possibilities of eloquence because he is conscious of his inchoate identity as a writer. He does not forsake its existence in the world – how could he when his just concluded narrative bursts with eloquent instances of the spoken word? How could he when the goal of his narrative has been freedom from the shackles of illusion, self-preoccupation, and isolation? Seeing that the act of narrative is bound up with the "rich babel" (*SA*, 112) of American oral expression, Invisible Man aspires to eloquence in his new profession (not career) as a writer. In that vocation, the techniques of spoken eloquence and the related forms of jazz and storytelling are exemplary points of reference for narrative. As a writer, Invisible Man continues to be a performer. He addresses his audience directly with the pronoun *you* as he has not done since the Prologue, where he made his defiant demand for attention. But now *you* seems more fraternal and intimate than aggressive and impersonal, even if ironically so, for now his irony seeks a positive response from readers.

As a performer, Invisible Man has been changed by the narrative act, by writing down his story; especially by symbolically reperforming his speeches and by the earlier experience of living that story and giving those speeches. Writing puts him in touch with his former performing voice, excites a more complex, inclusive sense of

identity, and connects him responsively to the world. So much so
that he leaves open the possibility that the "socially responsible"
role he'll soon emerge to try may involve the repursuit of eloquence
through the spoken word. And, indeed, his just completed memoir
is a writer's act of social responsibility, a recognition that "American society cannot define the role of the individual, or at least not
that of the *responsible* individual" (*GT*, 49).

In the Epilogue, the act of writing is informing and anticipatory
because it requires so much self-revelation. For this reason, Invisible Man's narrative of invisibility is an act of profound visibility.
And the visibility of his words on the page hastens his decision to
reenter the world. Moreover, he does not exaggerate the pleasures
of the written word. "So why do I write," he asks, "torturing
myself to put it down?" Because writing's disciplined contest with
self moves his will closer to action. "Without the possibility of
action, all knowledge comes to one labeled 'file and forget,' and I
can neither file nor forget" (437). Whereas throughout his time as
an orator, he used acts of speech to restrain his audience's urge to
action, now the act of writing commits him to action. The first
consequence of his new position is a resolve "to at least *tell* a few
people about it" (437) – about his journey to experience and
knowledge, about the possibility and necessity of action. Like
Emerson's *writing* on eloquence – like Douglass, Lincoln, and
Twain, Emerson was a preeminent public performer who infused
the written with the spoken word – Invisible Man's Epilogue calls
his potential participatory audience to action.

Invisible Man's career as a failed orator teaches him that he
must speak *to* us, his audience, in order to speak *for* us. And he
returns to that condition of eloquence in the profoundly rhetorical
question with which he ends: "Who knows but that on the lower
frequencies I speak for you?" A writer's communication with his
audience – citizens, some of whom may also be other writers –
may be an act of leadership. But, because of the nature of literature, narrative leadership is a symbolic act. Invisible Man, having
set himself free, encourages his readers to take similar action. He
does not attempt, as he has done presumptuously and blindly so
many times, to lead his audience but to make contact on an equal
individual basis. Everyone has a life to lead, a story to tell but not

necessarily a narrative to write. The last depends on craft and circumstances, personality, chance, and will, yet Invisible Man's question implicates every citizen in Ellison's call for a novel "fashioned as a raft of hope, perception and entertainment that might help keep us afloat as we tried to negotiate the snags and whirlpools that mark our nation's vascillating course toward and away from the democratic ideal" (xix). In the end, Invisible Man and Ellison float toward eloquence and the "possibility of action" on their respective narrative rafts of memoir and novel.

For his part, Invisible Man acknowledges and spells out the transforming effects of the act of narrative. As was the case with his speeches, his initial intention differs from the effect of his words. "Here I've set out to throw my anger into the world's face, but now that I've tried to put it all down the old fascination with playing a role returns, and I'm drawn upward again" (437). But the act of writing complicates and changes his idea of performance. His written words turn him back to social action as his spoken words propelled his audiences. The act of writing, "of trying to put it all down," sharpens his awareness of diversity and complexity, possibility and limitation, and leads him to accept the burden of love. "I have to love," he writes, "so I approach it [life] through division. So I denounce and I defend and I hate and I love" (438). At the level of conjunction and relationship, *and* replaces *but* as the rhythm and meaning of his words signal re-engagement with the world.

In his essays, Ralph Ellison proposes a reading of American fiction rooted in the idea and practice of democracy. What Invisible Man calls division is, in Ellison's view, essential if one is to understand and participate fully in American life, socially and culturally as well as politically. In "Twentieth Century Fiction and the Black Mask of Humanity," an essay written in 1946 when he was struggling with *Invisible Man*, Ellison asks why contemporary American fiction had failed to create "characters possessing the emotional, psychological and intellectual complexity which would allow them to possess and articulate a truly democratic world view?" (*SA*, 37). This is less a question than an assertion of the task Ellison sets for characters and narrators alike. Invisible Man's arduous self-reconstruction forces him to recognize the ambiguity and contradiction, as well as the possibilities inherent in the "principle on which the country was built" (*IM*, 433), its many violations, and in his own contrary and complementary impulses toward love and politics. In the Epilogue, the pursuit of narrative becomes the Declaration of Independence's pursuit of happiness as Invisible Man calls eloquently for reconsideration of the rights and responsibilities of democratic citizenship.

Formally too, Ellison's commitment to an American improvisatory vernacular rescues Invisible Man, namely, the Epilogue's embodiment of an open, responsive, literary text. Call-and-response turns the dialectic of words into Invisible Man's resolve to act, to emerge from his underground solitary confinement to play a socially responsible role. Together, his experience and narrative confirm the concept of eloquence. Invisible Man's failure as an orator and would-be African-American leader and his slow, painfully self-critical comprehension of that failure have "taught [him] something of the cost of being an individual who aspires to conscious eloquence" (*SA*, 117). And so he enacts a favorite Ellison proposition: that a work of art "is a social action in itself" (*SA*, 137). This in no way exalts the word over the world. Rather, it declares allegiance to both language and action and calls for collaboration between writer, narrator, and reader; between oral and literary techniques and traditions; between performance and composition.

For Ralph Ellison, the struggle with form is bound up with America. He is fascinated by his country and affirms its principles and possibilities in a complicated, mysterious, tender, satiric, vulnerable, and multifaceted way. Then and now, he refuses to leave the definition of the nation to those who misunderstand or underestimate the richness, complexity, and possibility inherent in its vernacular culture. Therefore, Ellison chooses to write a patriotic novel, but on his terms. "My problem," he has written, "is to affirm while resisting."[21] And he condemns and renounces many of his country's practices; this too is the essence of the patriot's role. As an American novelist and a Negro, he strives to influence the novel in somewhat the same way that the Civil Rights movement of the 1950s and 1960s set out to change the social and political character of American society. Who knows, to paraphrase Invisible Man's last lingering question, but on the "lower frequencies," Ellison's articulate, intellectual passion informed the struggles of the 1950s and 1960s? Who knows but that *Invisible Man* was a cultural catalyst for some of the energy and achievement of the civil rights movement?

Certainly, few values were more unfashionable among American intellectuals during the late 1940s and early 1950s than patriotism. For expressions of that attitude and tone, Ellison looked to the nineteenth century and discovered a sense of national complexity and responsibility, an experimental attitude appropriate to the metamorphoses taking place in *Invisible Man*. There, he declares, "the moral imperatives of American life that are implicit in the Declaration of Independence, the Constitution, and the Bill of Rights were a part of both the individual consciousness and the conscience of those writers who created what we consider our classic novels – Hawthorne, Melville, James, and Twain" (*GT*, 248).[22] Yet Ellison could not simply return to the aesthetic terms of the nineteenth-century novel when for him "every serious novel is, beyond its immediate thematic preoccupations, *a discussion of the craft*" and when "more than any other literary form the novel is obsessed with the impact of change upon personality" (*GT*, 240–1, 244; my emphasis) – and with the impact of social change upon literary form. Nor could he merely innovate because, for him, form for form's sake renounces the novelist's responsibilities to society. "The novel," he insists throughout the 1950s, "is bound up with the notion of nationhood" (*GT*, 242).

When Ellison contends that "the interests of art and democracy converge" and connects "the development of conscious, articulate citizens" to "the creation of conscious, articulate characters," he makes inextricable the evolving twin experiments of democracy and the novel. In his view, "resonant compositional centers" of fiction express the complexity of both the novel and American democratic society (*IM*, xviii, xix). For him the novelist's individual imagination responds to the flux of American life. According to Ellison's 1982 Introduction, Invisible Man already existed as an imaginary or, better, an imagined version of the "conscious, articulate citizen." Ellison did not so much invent him as fill in his character from the grain of his voice. And this is exactly Ellison's point about American society: There are countless articulate but invisible men and women in the nation's complex underground who profess "a certain necessary faith in human possibility before the next unknown" (*GT*, 319). Similar voices, yet to be identified and given palpable form in American fiction, excite Ellison's faith in the possibility of expressing that special American fluidity of class, culture, and personality. These variations on a volatile, seething, largely unheard and ignored eloquence spur Invisible Man's call for collaboration with Ellison and with us, his kin, at his narrative's end.

Finally, because of his symbolic performance in the Epilogue, Invisible Man merges social and personal impulses in "a single complex act" of narrative. When he writes *you*, he refers to Ellison as well as to potential and actual readers – after all, Ellison was his initial audience. In some sense, each sets the other free. What began as an act of " 'antagonistic cooperation' " (*SA*, 143) ends as a sympathetic, continuing dialectical act. Like the reader, Ellison is enjoined to talk back to Invisible Man. And he does. Moreover, his author's act of response builds on an earlier idea about the protean nature of fiction. Back in 1946, Ellison argued for the novel's potential as a social action and form catalytic to the continuing experiment of American democracy. "Once introduced into society," he wrote, "the work of art begins to pulsate with those meanings, emotions, ideas *brought to it by its audience* and over which the artist has but limited control" (*SA*, 38; my emphasis). Now, more than three decades later, Ellison strengthens his novelist's bill of rights with an amendment: The writer, before and after his act of composition, is audience to his work and has the same rights and responsibilities as the rest of us – equally and individually, in the name of eloquence and action, in the name of citizenship.

NOTES

1. Ralph Ellison, *Shadow and Act* (New York: Random House, 1964), p. 143. This volume will be cited hereafter as *SA*.

2. Ralph Ellison, *Going to the Territory* (New York: Random House, 1986), p. 59. This volume will be cited hereafter as *GT.*

3. Invisible Man refers to *Notes from the Underground* at the beginning of his Prologue, and revises and revoices Dostoievsky's narrator's perspective in order to express his African-American voice and condition. Unlike Dostoievsky, Ellison does not intervene and write an ironic footnote as apologia for his character/narrator. Invisible Man consciously plays off Dostoievsky and his underground man in order to imply that he will go to both traditions of the vernacular, literary and folk, in order to become a writer in what Ellison repeatedly calls this "crazy country."

4. For Ellison's further comment on his view of Negro leadership at the time of writing *Invisible Man*, see *Going to the Territory*, pp. 44–5, 59–60, 62–6, 125–33, 144, 317–18.

5. Both Larry Neal and Albert Murray have found evidence of musical form in *Invisible Man*. In "Ellison's Zoot Suit," *Ralph Ellison: A Collection of Critical Essays*, ed. John Hersey (Englewood Cliffs, N.J.: Prentice-Hall, 1974), Neal argues that from the entrance of Louis Armstrong's "Black and Blue" in the Prologue, "the subsequent narrative and all of the action which follows can be read as one long blues solo" (p. 71). And in *The Omni-Americans* (New York: Outerbridge, 1970), Murray claims that "Ellison had taken an everyday twelve-bar blues tune . . . and scored it for full orchestra" (p. 167). Likewise, in his biography, *The Craft of Ralph Ellison* (Cambridge, Mass.: Harvard University Press, 1980), pp. 78–104, Robert G. O'Meally discusses jazz and folk songs in *Invisible Man*.

6. Ishmael Reed, Quincy Troupe, and Steve Cannon, "The Essential Ellison: An Interview," *Y'Bird*, (1978):132.

7. *The Journals and Miscellaneous Notebooks of Ralph Waldo Emerson*, Vol. IX, 1843–7, ed. Ralph H. Orth and Alfred Ferguson (Cambridge, Mass.: Belknap Press, 1971), pp. 425–6; my emphasis.

8. Ellison discusses the impact of Kenneth Burke's "The Rhetoric of Hitler's Battle" and his own notion of "symbolic action" in the *Y'Bird* interview, "The Essential Ellison," pp. 148, 156.

9. Quoted by R. W. B. Lewis, *The American Adam* (Chicago: University of Chicago Press, 1955), p. 6.

10. Booker T. Washington, *Up From Slavery* (New York: A. L. Burt, 1901), p. 224.

11. See W. E. B. DuBois's discussion of Washington in chap. 3 of *The Souls of Black Folk*, "Of Mr. Booker T. Washington and Others" (1903; rpt. New York: Fawcett Publications, 1961), p. 48.

12. And in the South, opposition to Washington was voiced almost at once. A few months after Washington delivered his Atlanta Address, a young black scholar named John Hope told a Nashville audience in public repudiation of Washington's stance: "Now, catch your breath, for I am going to use an adjective: I am going to say we demand social equality. In this republic, we shall be less than freemen, if we have a whit less than that which thrift, education, and honor afford other freemen"; quoted by Edgar A. Toppin in *A Biographical History of Blacks in America Since 1528* (New York: David McKay, 1971), p. 165.

13. From his student days at Tuskegee in the mid-1930s, Ellison was fascinated by Eliot's and Joyce's use of "ancient myth and ritual." "But," he commented in a *Paris Review* interview, "it took me a few years to realize that the myths and rites which we find functioning in our everyday lives could be used in the same way" (*SA*, 174).

14. In his long account of the Third National Negro Congress, "A Congress Jim Crow Didn't Attend," *New Masses* (May 14, 1940), Ellison makes some fascinating observations on the different styles and perspectives of those aspiring to Negro leadership from the left. This and other Ellison articles for *New Masses* confirm his long-standing interest in the question of Negro leadership in the United States.

15. Ralph Ellison, "Remembering Richard Wright," *Going to the Territory* (New York: Random House, 1986), pp. 208–9.

16. His words recall the metaphors of "sittin' on high" and "de rulin' chair" in *Their Eyes Were Watching God* (1937; rpt. Urbana: University of Illinois Press, 1978), pp. 31, 54. Like Janie Crawford, Invisible Man eventually – in his case, he involuntarily and unceremoniously descends – rejects such simplistic, hierarchical notions of success and self-fulfillment. But for a long time, he clings to the texts of Booker T. Washington and Benjamin Franklin. For a good discussion of Douglass's complex role in *Invisible Man* and Invisible Man's misunderstanding of Douglass's vocation as a writer, see Robert B. Stepto's *From Behind the Veil* (Urbana: University of Illinois Press, 1979), pp. 172–5, 185–90. Stepto's argument hinges on the idea that a number of African-American narratives are polar works of immersion or ascent. In the sense that he authors his autobiography, Invisible Man's account of his past misconception of Douglass reveals his comprehension of Douglass's achievement as a writer. Douglass also tried his hand at fiction, and there, too, as Stepto argues in "Storytelling in Early Afro-American Fiction: Frederick Douglass's 'The Heroic Slave,'" *Georgia Review* 36, no. 2 (Summer 1982):355–68, pursued what Stepto calls the "quest for freedom and literacy."

17. Like Invisible Man, Frederick Douglass first spoke his story and then wrote it, in his case in three successive, evolving autobiographies: *Narrative of the Life of Frederick Douglass, an American Slave, Written by Himself* (1845), *My Bondage and My Freedom* (1855), and *The Life and Times of Frederick Douglass* (1892).

18. *Journals and Miscellaneous Notebooks,* pp. 425–6.

19. Ibid., p. 426.

20. James Joyce, *A Portrait of the Artist as a Young Man* (1916; rpt. with revision, New York: Viking, 1961), p. 247.

21. Letter from Ralph Ellison to the author, August 12, 1983.

22. Ellison was reading James's fiction extensively when he began to write *Invisible Man,* and acknowledges a debt to the aesthetic and moral complexity with which James pursued the American theme. Yet Ellison found James largely deaf to the democratic commitment to "make the illiterate and inarticulate eloquent enough so that the educated and more favorably situated will recognize wisdom and honor and charity, heroism and capacity for love when found in humble speech and dress" (*GT,* 273). For Ellison's discussion of James, see also *GT,* 249–54, 262–73, 313–16.

4

Ralph Waldo Ellison: Anthropology, Modernism, and Jazz

BERNDT OSTENDORF

THOUGH a highly conscious artist who is eloquent about the meaning of his art, Ralph Waldo Ellison is, in his own words, not a systematic thinker, certainly not one with a blueprint or program. Least of all does he believe in radical utopias or pious certainties. And his work shows a healthy distrust of simple answers. Hence, any attempt to chart a map of his thinking about American literature and culture is doomed to a measure of failure. For he belongs, like his protagonist in *Invisible Man,* to the tradition of American tinkerers, and he is, like his namesake Ralph Waldo Emerson, a manipulator of words – the French would call him a *bricoleur* of language.

And yet, the cumulative evidence of his stories, his essays, his novel, and his carefully choreographed interviews, all of which will be treated here as one universe of discourse, allows us to identify certain recurrent strategies of thinking, typical scenarios and interactions, arguments, and scripts. If we were to divide aesthetic paradigms and their attendant world views into those based on *being* and those based on *becoming,* Ellison would favor the latter and would therfore opt for ritual, open-endedness, latency, ambivalence, and antistructure.[1] His meanings are therefore temporary and transient, or, to use his own word, *experimental.* His answers are of the yes-but sort, shot through with disclaimers and contradictions that mirror, condense, and clarify (but rarely resolve) the political and social ambiguities of black American existence in the New World.

Though Ellison favors dynamic paradigms, in his artistic practice he may be said to have written himself into a modernist deadlock. His work, in particular his novel, has become an awesome prison house circumscribed by expectations of more and better things to come. This contradiction between open, fluid, improvisational social ideals and intimidating writerly practice needs to be elaborated. Ellison's fluid anthropology and his stern Modernism are at odds or, perhaps, in constant negotiation. They could be seen as thesis and antithesis, and jazz might be the synthesis.

I consider here three encompassing frames that give meaning and direction both to his work and to his opinions. None of these frames takes on the hard contours of a program to which Ellison would at all times be loyal. Rather, he plays with them or improvises on them, as a jazz musician would use chord progressions. Modifying Kenneth Burke's metaphor, he "dances" in and around these frames. And both jazz and dance are, of course, key traditions of black expressive culture with deep meaning for Ellison's art.

The first frame is a ritual theory of culture and society that derives its vocabulary from symbolic action and anthropology. This frame includes and structures Ellison's ideas on black folklore. The second or Modernist frame informs his ideas about personal and collective literary tradition, as well as his views on the function of the novel. Modernism also influences his ideas concerning the antinomian function of black American art in white American society. Modernism grew out of the ruling episteme of the late nineteenth century, put on the agenda by Marx, Nietzsche, and Freud, whose interest focused broadly on the latency of the world and on strategies to bring the hitherto invisible into view. Although for many European Modernist artists this was an episteme of crisis and decline, Ellison would read it as one of *possibility*. One of his root metaphors, after all, combines latency and possibility: *hibernation*. The third frame is that of jazz. Here I refer to jazz not only as one of several discrete genres of music but as a pervasive cultural style. Louis Armstrong, first in Ellison's hall of fame, allegedly once said, "What we play is life."[2] For Ellison, jazz represents a working out of an American vernacular, a national style. In fact, for him, all American culture, including baseball, is "jazz-shaped." Jazz is an example and chief exhibit for Ellison's conception of a pluralist culture that, as opposed to bounded social and political systems of power, knows no frontiers, whether marked by color or by genes. Of these three frames, jazz is the most inclusive, for it incorporates and synthesizes the contradictions of the previous two. Not only is jazz a symbolic action, it is the true musical idiom of Modernism.

Ritual: The Dancing of an Attitude

Ellison's many references to Lord Raglan and the Cambridge School of ritual, and also to Kenneth Burke, indicate an abiding interest in dramaturgical metaphors to describe cultural and social processes. These thinkers conceived of the social sphere as an arena where the individual uses cultural resources and personal talent not only to master the game of life but even to transcend personal or social limitations. Though Ellison makes a great deal of the term *consciousness*, his characters and individuals are rarely mere *Kopfmenschen*, cerebral constructs or mental abstractions. Long before any theories of body language were current, Ellison played with the embodiment of language, on the one hand, and the body and its signals, on the other. In this sense, Ellison's understanding of the meaning of style is anthropological rather than narrowly technical. For him, style refers to the handling of language as well as to the handling of the body: "It has been said that Escudero could recapitulate the history and spirit of the Spanish dance with a simple arabesque of his fingers."[3] Vernacular dance, vernacular language, and vernacular music represent for this high cultural Modernist a total body of culture. And Ellison wants to translate that energy into the organized discipline of his art. Discrete items of black culture – say blues by Jimmy Rushing – are for him synecdoche, metonymy, and metaphor of the cumulative historical experience of black people in the United States. Jazz, dance, and language all partake of a total world view and a total way of life. Hence, one of the harshest estimates that Ellison ever made of Richard Wright was that "he knew very little about jazz and didn't even know how to dance."[4]

Transformations

Ellison's interest in becoming over being and in open-ended possibility rather than in closed systems explains his preoccupation with transformations, metamorphosis, and hibernation. Afro-Americans, he writes, have been kept in a state of alert, biding their time, poised in a situation of watchful waiting and suspension of final judgment. Their being cut off from the closed world of white power has its own ironic advantages, says Ellison. As Diderot states, the lord may have the title, but the bondsman is in possession of the things of life. Or as Hegel suggests, the former is limited by the finite limitations of power, whereas the latter has before him infinite possibilities and may live in a world of hope. His advantage is described by Kenneth Burke in a most Ellisonian manner: "We win by capitalizing on our debts, by turning our liabilities into assets, by using our burden as a basis of insights," thus fooling or subverting power structures, a strategy of which the protagonist of *Invisible Man* is a shrewd advocate.[5]

His profound concern with states of becoming and with crisis points of the life cycle lets Ellison choose as heroes youngsters and adolescents who are on the verge of breaking into responsibility. His interest in heroes in general centers not so much on their power or status as on their *transformations*. In dramatic terms, Ellison recounts a storytelling ritual in a barbershop in which a local black hero is extolled:

> His crimes, his lives, his outrages, his adventures, his *transformations*, his moments of courage, his heroism, buffooneries, defeats and triumphs are recited with each participant joining in. And this catalogue soon becomes a brag, a very exciting chant, celebrating the *metamorphosis* which this individual in question *underwent* within the limited circumstances available to us.[6]

Ellison's interest in transformations and metamorphosis recalls the anthropological debate on *liminality* (Victor Turner) and *boundary maintenance* (Frederic Barth). These concepts refer to rites of passage, that is, to the transformation from youth to adulthood and to that imaginary or real social line that separates the self and the group from others. Both liminality and boundary maintenance have been particularly pressing concerns for adolescent blacks, Ellison's favorite heroes. Ellison loves rituals in which color and status are at cross purposes; he also pokes fun at the paranoid racist fear that one drop of black blood might soil the mighty white race.

98

On a more pragmatic level, Ellison relates his *positionality* vis-à-vis America and black culture to his place of birth and to growing up in a state of the Union that was then undergoing rapid change. In an address honoring Richard Wright, Ellison complained that few critics had paid attention to their places of origin. Wright hailed from Mississippi, Ellison from Oklahoma City. Oklahoma, which was admitted to the Union only a few years prior to his birth, was a place on the American margin, a frontier state defined by a frontier culture and outlook. Within that fronter life, blacks were clearly an undecided or marginal issue (Oklahoma had not bothered to regulate its laws and attitudes concerning blacks), in contrast to Mississippi, where the presence of blacks *as victims* defined, structured, and *closed* the social system. Ellison's sense of self, place, and time, as well as his particular cultural perspectives, are defined by the frontier paradigm, that transitional space with its options and tensions between freedom and necessity, safety and danger, liberty and restraint, order and disorder.

In Ellison's fiction, this frontier paradigm of liminality is a central metaphor for those characters who will not surrender to society's weighty pressures. After Tod's death, the protagonist of *Invisible Man* experiences a painful burst of perception: He notices certain Harlem youngsters who speak "a jived up transitional language full of country glamour, think transitional thoughts" (355). The novel's Prologue and Epilogue could be read, both in form and in content, as essays on liminality and transition. The protagonist defines his current situation as hibernation in a cellar located on the border between white and black neighborhoods. His time and space are liminal. The underground situates him at the lower, invisible margin of the vertical social order, with free power from an unwitting power company to light his underground. The underground is Ellison's encompassing metaphor for the locus of black culture in America, both in the sense of providing the *basis* (Marx) or the *mudsill,* according to certain southern senators of the 1940s and 1950s, but also in the sense of the guerrilla notion of an invisible underground that may at any moment subvert the mainstream, particularly the mainstream of color. Playing Louis Armstrong records in a coal cellar, to which he has descended, the protagonist has finally come into possession of his identity and consciousness. Hence his descent, as Ellison reminds us, is also a classic ascent.

Ellison has often insisted on the importance of the black presence for the American body politic. In his essay "What America Would Be Like Without Blacks," he states that in a cleansed state America would probably succumb to a "moral slobbism" (*GT*, 111). Here Ellison shrewdly applies the second law of thermodynamics to social systems; it says that homogeneous, closed systems are incapable of moral and artistic renewal. Creative change issues rarely from the center of a consensus, from the structurally hard core of a majority or from within rigid power structures. Closed structures and systems are interested in maintaining the norm, the habit, the done thing, the boundary. This is why ethnic pluralism and diversity are necessary and why so-called minority groups are essential for questioning rigid norms and for activating their renewal. Such a marginal or transitional position requires a special vision and a special talent for interactions. What Ralph Waldo Emerson and W. E. B. DuBois called *double consciousness* Ellison prefers to call a *double vision*. This revision of Emerson's and DuBois's concepts provides a key example, in fact, of Ellison's turning an apparent liability into an asset. According to Ellison, the look across the fence increases sociability and tolerance, whereas the single vision is in danger of becoming paranoid. Such an artistic *perspective by incongruity* is well known in American ethnic writing.[7] Such a double vision trains the ability and willingness to assume the second self and look at oneself as if from the outside. Double vision implies an acceptance of dialogue and of a plurality of voices. It is a matter of existential survival for Ellison's heroes not to accept the last word, whether it comes from the family, the church, the union, or the Brotherhood.

Linkage and complimentarity: call and response

An important word in Ellison's vocabulary is the conjunction *and*. "I was taken very early with a passion to link together all I loved within the Negro community and all those things I felt in the world which lay beyond." The *and* establishes linkage, but not merely in an additive fashion. It may unite *and* separate, yet it never stops dialogue. It controls and maintains a precarious balance between union and division, order and disorder. Ellison's *ands* are dialectical, combative, antiphonal, and always dialogical. A quick look at his essay titles ought to make this clear: "The Seer *and* the Seen," "Change the Joke *and* Slip the Yoke," "The World *and* the Jug," "Hidden Name *and* Complex Fate," "Some Questions *and* Some Answers," and most obviously, *Shadow and Act*. Furthermore the blues are described as being "tragic *and* comic" and the protagonist of *Invisible Man* preaches "so I denounce *and* I defend, *and* I love *and* I hate." The novel begins with *I* and ends with *you;* hence it fills the space of the *and* between protagonist and reader; it provides the narrative linkage.[8]

Michail Bahktin's theory of the novel was inspired by Russian folklore. Ellison draws equally on black folk sources. Black folk storytelling uses the narrative strategy of *signifying* that is embodied in the figure of the trickster. The trickster, who is a prominent character in many folk cultures all over the world, is essentially a figure of ambivalence, openness, and fluidity.[9] Storytelling and the trickster figure are generically involved with each other, the one depending on the other. Not only are some of our best stories by and about tricksters, but storytelling itself partakes of the existential ambiguity of this central figure. In this context, it is significant that certain stories in black and other folklores are told as lies. The label *lie* is not only the visa that permits their being told at large with impunity, but also a licensing mechanism and credibility ruse that – on a deep level – inspires both folk stories and fiction. The French call fiction *mentir vrai*, lying truthfully. Truth *and* lie. It is unsurprising, then, that both master plans of Ellison's first novel were based on such "lies" about tricksters. Initially he had planned a novel on flying (the story "Flying Home," 1944, is an offshoot of that attempt), but he ended up writing one on invisibility.

The strategy of signifying pervades *Invisible Man*. It crops up at strategic places in the novel, as when the protagonist addresses the implied reader: "Let me be honest with you – a feat which, by the way, I find of the utmost difficulty" (*IM* 461). Lying or truth, signifying is also the ambivalent basis of the folk tale about Sweet the Monkey who "could make himself invisible." Ellison heard this tale from one Leo Gurley while collecting folklore for the Federal Writers Project (and there is a moral in this as well):

> I hope to God to kill me if this aint the truth. All you got to do is go down to Florence, South Carolina, and ask most anybody you meet and they'll tell you its the truth.

Legitimation by hearsay is the basis of all legend and rumor, but it identifies and makes visible *any* narrative construction of reality. In their very presentation, such stories constitute *and* deconstruct themselves. Sweet the Monkey – and this is not his real name, as the storyteller hastens to inform us – could make himself invisible. He acquired this talent by "cutting open a black cat, taking out its heart, climbing up a tree backwards and cursing God." These voodoo formulas tie in with other folk traditions such as European witchcraft or its trickster heritage. This is a world upside down, where fair is foul and foul is fair. Beginning with Lucifer's reversal of Godhead, it invokes the radical "other." Its ambivalence is the existential basis of all storytelling magic: "Black is . . . and black ain't" says the preacher in *Invisible Man*'s Prologue. Gurley continues:

> Once they found a place he'd looted with footprints leading away from it and they decided to try and trap im. This was bout sun up and they followed his footprints all that day. They followed them till sundown when he come partly visible. It was red and the sun was shining on the trees and they waited till they saw his shadow. That was the last of Sweet-the-Monkey. They never did find his body and right after that I came up here. That was about five years ago. My brother was down there last year and they said they think Sweet done come back. *But they caint be sho because he wont let hisself be seen.*[10]

Again we get the typical disclaimer, a withdrawal behind the smoke screen of fantasy.

One obvious trickster figure in the novel, Peetie Wheatstraw, is both a manipulator of words and a blues singer, but we should pay attention not only to what he says but also to what he does. This street poet from the black folk tradition is, we are led to assume, taking blueprints to the shredder. This symbolic act encapsulates his trickster ethos: He destroys paper stories, literate fictions. Ellison has a bit of fun here. It used to be a widely accepted dogma in cultural theory that literate cultures wipe out oral traditions.

Legions of folklorists were motivated by this fear. Wheatstraw's act turns this theory on its head. Again we have this play on reversals: It is and it ain't, says the preacher in the dream sequence. Or as Brer Rabbit has it, "Dis am life; some go up and some go down."

The tragic sense of ambivalence in kinship relations is articulated in the dream sequence of the Prologue. A black mother kills the white father of her sons in order to save him from being more brutally murdered by them. Her comment: "I have learned to live with ambivalence." Or take Trueblood, who is literally true to his blood to the extent of becoming his own son-in-law or father-in-law, whose daughter is his mate and whose wife his mother-in-law. Trueblood ends up singing the blues and accepting that he is who he is. Not surprisingly Ellison has repeatedly defined the blues as an "art of ambiguity." Even the book of history, the rational blueprint for future action, becomes doubtful when the protagonist asks rhetorically: "What if history is a gambler?" thus echoing the folk formula: "Heads I win, tails you lose." (Which Ellison quotes in his reply to Howe.)

Ellison's pervasive use of what I would call trickster strategies and scenarios fleshes out his understanding of human symbolic action. At the bottom of these recurrent strategies, there is a belief that there is something deeply antirepressive both in the accumulated historical wisdom of black folk and in the African heritage of black culture. For example, jazz players were often accused of playing "not quite on the beat" or "dirty" by those who favored a strict adherence to "lines and dots." Born in enforced labor and perfected in the freedom of play, this antirepressive attitude has matured into a full-blown aesthetic, one that denies system, closure, purity, abstract design and thrives on improvisation, off-beat rhythms, syncopation, or what Ellison called "the sudden turns, the shocks, the swift changes of pace (all jazz shaped) that serve to remind us that the *world is ever unexplored*" (*GT*, 109–10). Clearly, the denial of closure is embodied by *Invisible Man*'s very form, which has irritated those readers who, instead of the signifying of the Epilogue and Prologue, wanted a "well-made" beginning, middle, and end.

The dialogic principle and the trickster ethos come together in

Ellison's notion of masking or of the second self. In order to enter into different styles, codes, and world views, one must be an actor, a changer of roles, a wearer of masks. The theme of masking has two angles:

1. We must be able to wear the mask in order to assume the second self and tolerate the other.
2. We must be able to manipulate masks for survival.

For Ellison, the wearing of a mask is no black monopoly; in fact, the American identity is based on what he calls a *joke*. With Yeatsian overtones he writes:

> For the ex-colonials, the declaration of an American identity meant the assumption of a mask, and it imposed not only the discipline of a national self-consciousness, it gave Americans an ironic awareness of the joke that always lies between appearances and reality, between the discontinuity of social tradition and that sense of the past which clings to the mind. And perhaps even an awareness of the joke that society is man's creation, not God's.[11]

Those believing in pure authenticity or in the existence of ontological finality denounce masking as inauthentic, as a denial of identity; and thus, of course, they fall for the joke. On the other hand, if one accepts masking not only as a temporary necessity but as a constant existential fact, and therefore as a resource, then even the role playing of Louis Armstrong may hide deeper secrets. We should go one step further and agree with radical anthropologists that only those who assume the second self are truly capable of democracy and humanity (Dürr, Geertz). Role playing and the assumption of the other mask indicate a political credo, namely, an anti-imperialistic and anticolonialistic willingness to begin to understand the other, though it be in stereotype or in unavoidable initial ignorance. We recall Ellison's evaluation of Faulkner: He began with the stereotype but then took pains to discover the humanity behind it.

It is crucial to note that the trickster ethos or the notion of masking should not be misunderstood in the context of ready-made stereotypes that hold that all blacks are typically tricksters. Though the trickster is a distinct black folk type, he is clearly a character in a global literary pantheon. The trickster in America embodies what Ellison has called the "diversity of American life with its extreme fluidity and openness." Many readers will not share this optimistic evaluation of America's promise; for them Ellison makes too much of the positive virtues of America's openness. Where many black Americans have seen limitation, he sees possibilities; when others would worship wounds, he would rather explore the not yet known and see in mere survival enough ground for celebration.

Many of his critics have called this stance a copout: making the best of a bad deal. There is, depending on one's position or ulterior motives, some truth in such criticism. Yet, his detractors ignore the radicalism of the Ellisonian philosophical anthropology, which refuses to posit simple utopias of being. Ellison puts more faith in the energy of day-to-day combat and believes in accumulating wisdom in the here and now. He is a radical American pragmatist, as it were. Others have faulted Ellison's work for the lack of a clear political commitment and have been irritated by his ideological agnosticism, which makes it hard for them to reduce his politics to a platform. Those whose sense of truth is shaped by a simple faith in realism – Nietzsche called this the *dogma of immaculate perception* – are often bothered by his antimimetic aesthetic. Old-fashioned Marxists in particular bridle at his aesthetics. And from a stable ideological center, his views may easily be called *conservative*. A penchant for mediation, for the reconciliation of opposites, and for the maintenance of an ambivalent state of balance between order and chaos would, according to Karl Mannheim's typology of ideologies, fall into a conservative archetype of thought. But these categories work only if and when there is a firm historicist frame, which according to Ellison – or Lévi-Strauss – is merely another transitory myth. Again: "What if history is a gambler?"

Ellison's radicalism is of a different sort: It doubts the very ideological beliefs on which radical solutions rest. It rejects all closed systems that speak with a single voice. Ellison speaks forcefully against any colonization and against any systems of thought that are too rigidly schematic. Yet, Ellison's ideological ambivalence does not lead to mere relativism or to a rejection of values per se. In his social philosophy he stands in an American moral tradition that includes Emerson, Whitman, James, Dewey, and Mead.

Language and symbolic action

How do a ritual theory of culture, an interest in transformations, and a concern with the dialogic principle translate into poetic practice? For Ellison, language is both form and content, medium and message. Language is not only in itself a form of reality, but also a way of working through reality, a way of working things out. It is, in and by itself, a creative force and an agency and repository of wisdom. Language is a special form of artistic production and, in the words of Karl Marx, *practical consciousness*. And poetry is the performance of such language: symbolic action. Its smithy is the ongoing vernacular process. Ellison would agree with the linguist Jespersen, who used to say that proper grammar and good style are the product of generations of illiterate speakers. Ellison is concerned with the American vernacular as precisely such a working out of social and cultural conflicts; it is also a working out of an American identity. For him, the American vernacular is involved in an unending fight to achieve a better fit between word and thing, between the promise and the reality of its Constitution; hence it is a deeply moral agency with particular relevance for the discourse in race relations. As much as Adam Smith believed in the invisible hand of the free market system, Ellison puts his faith in the invisible and collective hand of the vernacular in a free society. But he is not a facile folk enthusiast who believes that the folk can do no wrong. After all, he came to folklore through literature; he discovered its potential, he says, because he had become a literary person by breaking through the horizon of a mere folk consciousness. Ellison insists on the need for transcendence from the unconscious rituals of a folk world to the expansive level of individualistic American freedom. This scenario is not based on a stratified notion of culture. His is a non-hegemonial theory of cultural influence – again, a radical departure from previous assumptions. An earlier theory assumed that folklore had seeped down from the culture bearers to the plebs and that folk songs were the residue of an operatic or *Lied* tradition. In the American context, this tacit belief translated into George Pullen Jackson's theory that spirituals were essentially white church songs sung badly by blacks.[12] If today black vernacular forms are no longer studied as a pathological offshoot of white culture, we should credit Ellison, who challenged these assumptions long before the cultural nationalism of the sixties.[13]

Modernism

As a literary phenomenon, Modernism loosely describes a period of heightened consciousness (and self-consciousness) that gathers in its fold many of the authors Ellison names as his ancestors: Eliot, Hemingway, Joyce, and Malraux. "In or about December 1910 human character changed," wrote Virginia Woolf, and Ezra Pound, everybody's literary coach, peptalked his artist friends into "making it new." With aesthetic changes came a new social role for art: It was seen by the artists themselves partly as a diagnosis of crisis, partly as a new transcendence. Diagnosis in the sense of Marx, Freud, and Nietzsche laying bare the invisible deep structures beneath the visible surface of things. Transcendence in the sense of T. S. Eliot, who advocated the return to older myths and rituals (and folklore) to combat the "chaos of modern history." Crisis and diagnosis inform the logic of discovery inherent in Modernism; therapy and transcendence inform the logic of demonstration. Art as a kind of writing cure: The imagination is itself a utopian sphere, and the poetic imagination helps to liberate text and reader from the bondage of history. With belief systems in general collapsed, the self becomes unhinged and is in perpetual search of alternatives, new frontiers, other worlds. Hence change itself is the hero of Modernism, and time is its keeper. In formal terms, this translates into a sophisticated handling of narrative, into a metaphorical complexity and a play of paradoxes; and the general absence of security results in a new intimacy between author and protagonist, on the one hand, and hero and reader, on the other.

Ellison is no mere follower of Modernism, but reconstructs its general purpose within a black historical consciousness and structure of feeling. Surely the inner history of black literature has followed its own logic, in counterpoint to the mainstream of American literature. While nineteenth-century white heroes such as Huck Finn or Ishmael were in flight from the body politic, lighting out for the territory or going in search of the primitive, Frederick Douglass fought against a primitive ascription and for a place within that very body politic. Much later, Claude McKay protested against exclusion from the "white house." The structure of black experience generates its own desires, topics, themes, and formal conventions, which, in comparison with the dominant American literary trends, seem traditional simply because blacks had to fight older American battles of self-liberation all over again. Heinrich Heine spoke of the "traditionalism of the excluded."

Hence Ellison's Modernism is certainly not one of white alienation or *anomie* caused by disgust with the world. "I'm not a separatist," he has said. "The imagination is integrative. That's how you make the new — by putting something else with what you've got. And I'm unashamedly an American integrationist."[14] This is indeed hard to swallow for critics driven by either white angst or black anger. Ellison's insistence on linkage, dialogue, and complementarity and his pragmatic American optimism are not quite on the beat and not in tune with the Modernist theme song. Using Ellisonian mocking metaphors, one might say that he was inspired by the Modernist *ancestors*, but that his and his *relatives'* cultural experience runs on its own black track.

Like his chosen ancestors, however, Ellison practices a literature of consciousness as a value that deserves to be maximized. Indeed, consciousness gives value to unconsciously lived lives. In Ellison's words: "It might sound arrogant to say so, but writers, poets, help create or reveal hidden realities by asserting their existence" (*GT*, 288). "I do not find it a strain to point to the heroic component of our experience, for these seem to me truths which we have long lived by but which we must not recognize consciously."[15] Art, in his words, represents not only a special form of creation but also a realm of liberation. Therefore he criticized Wright for excluding from his work the possibility of his own self-creation as a successful writer and for denying his characters the chance of consciousness that he himself had. Ellison sees literature as a radical alternative to artlessness and chaos (in Eliot's sense of that word) or to confusion that issues from ignorance. Whereas Wright's chief curse was the evil of racism, Ellison's pet peeve is ignorance, particularly when it is self-imposed and self-perpetuated. The appropriate generic choices were, therefore, in Wright's case tragedy, in Ellison's case comedy.

The *telos* of comedy is peace. Surely Ellison embraces democracy, pluralism, and tolerance as ultimate values, which shine from his work. This basic attitude embodies a concept of culture that is partly Modernist, partly black American. Ellison has a deep commitment to the invisible hand of culture as a symbolic system of checks and balances and a way of honing and shaping experience, all of which works itself out in language. He writes a very conscious, Modernist prose. Indeed, in his fiction he aims for an almost hypertrophied literariness and for a self-conscious network of *literary* quotation and *folk* allusion. Those who tire of his literary signifying may call him an overachiever, for he crosses semantic wires wherever possible and he delights in confusing those readers who want the strong authorial hand. He cannot bypass a potential pun that lies buried in language and would rather let his protagonist have a bad one than none at all (the pun on Brother Wrestrum's name, for example). Likewise, rather than avoid the politically charged language, academic and otherwise, that is often applied to blacks, Ellison exploits the various linguistic modes precisely for their playfulness and rich ambiguities. What for many bourgeois or political activists is a badge of inferiority – black folk culture – becomes a resource for this Modernist. He attempts to re-create the full range of black talk in terms of Modernist contextuality, which amounts to what Roman Jakobson called the strengthening of the *poetic function* of such language. Whereas Eliot and Joyce achieved poetic contextuality by using myth as a structural scaffolding and as a way of ordering the "chaos of modern history," Ellison mockingly invites the country cousin of myth, black folklore, into the salon of Modernist intertextuality. For him the black vernacular holds a store of repressed values that need to be made conscious through literacy. "When I listen to a folk story," he says, "I'm looking for what it conceals as well as what it states" (*GT*, 289).

Ellison's understanding of black folklore and what it conceals or reveals ties in with Clifford Geertz's notion of *thick description*. Geertz sees culture as a complex, thick web in which people enmesh themselves; they are, as it were, "entangled in stories."

Ellison seeks out these complex webs, makes connections, and unites the elements of black and white culture. Therefore, he is irritated by stereotyping formulas, whether advanced by white sociologists or black radicals: "I don't deny that these sociological formulas are drawn from life, but I do deny that they define the complexity of Harlem." There is something else, and "it is 'that something else' that challenges the sociologist who ignores it." Ellison's complex notion of white–black interaction does not find favor with white liberals or black radicals; in advocating a reading of American history that denies simple, separate genealogies, Ellison is in the Nietzschean sense *untimely,* and therefore without a constituency. He insists instead on a mutual, complex fate.

Jazz Aesthetics: Make It New, But Not Quite on the Beat

Ellison accepts the discipline implied in the slogan "make it new" but rejects the cultural pessimism of his Modernist ancestors. One explanation for his special optic lies, I believe, in his understanding of jazz as more than a form of musical entertainment. Eliot in his notorious essay "Ulysses, Order and Myth" had called for myth to replace moribund historical frames of reference. For Ellison there is no need for therapy or replacement. Jazz, blues, spirituals, and black folk religion have always provided the rituals that give order to the chaos of black experience. The problem is that these forms, though crucial to black American and general American culture, were (often by blacks as well as whites) denied, rejected, and suppressed – invisible. In the history of jazz, the tangle of black–white relations is particularly complex, but also paradigmatic for an understanding of what makes American culture what it is. Jazz also represents a testimony to a black coming of age in American culture: It announces the break into audibility and visibility, and it marks a black appropriation not only of the instruments, techniques, and strategies of music making but also of the public sphere and the market. Jazz represents also a striking through the mask of Stephen Foster minstrelsy. It constitutes an act of what Robert Stepto in a felicitous phrase calls *self-authentication.*[16] All of this may sound as if Ellison considers jazz to be a purely black creation. It is in his view rather a hybrid, a creole, a fusion of heterogeneous dialogues from the folk traditions of blacks and whites. The marching band of the German *Turnverein* in New Orleans, society orchestras, honky-tonk, and ragtime went into its making; and many of the first jazz artists received instruction from French or German music teachers, as Ellison did from Dr. Ludwig Hebestreit. Jazz therefore is a fitting paradigm for Ellison's understanding of the multiethnic American musical vernacular. Though not a friend of current jazz radicals, he would probably agree with jazz saxophonist and scholar Archie Shepp, who told Amiri Baraka:

> But jazz is American reality. Total reality. The jazz musician is like a reporter, an aesthetic journalist of America. Those white people who used to go to those bistros in New Orleans etc. thought they were listening to nigger music, but they weren't, they were listening to American music. Even today those white people who go slumming on the Lower East Side may not know it, but they are listening to American music. . . . The Negro contribution, his gift to America.[17]

Jazz is the only purely *American* cultural creation, which shortly after its birth became America's most important cultural export. The Army newspaper *Stars and Stripes* featured an article during the Korean War that told the story of a North Korean (i.e., Communist) soldier who had a record of Charlie Parker, "Bird of Paradise," among his possessions. One reason for the international success of this music is that jazz is the true idiom of American Modernism. Let me elaborate on this assumption, which, I submit, is also Ellison's. Jazz emerged as a distinct type of music in that period of innovation from about 1890 to 1920 that Paul Valéry heralded – and his words fit jazz very well: "We should be ready for such great innovations in all of art that invention itself will be changed and perhaps lead to a magic transformation of the concept of art itself." During those years, America was in a privileged situation not only to observe the meeting of many European vernacular cultures but also to witness their contact with the Afro-American – mostly rural – traditions in America's frontier cities: New Orleans, Kansas City, Oklahoma City, Chicago. Thus jazz emerged not in structurally strong cultural centers such as Boston and Philadelphia, but in southern and western urban centers that allowed a maximum of fluidity and contact. Here an eclecticism was made possible, which meant not only a new artistic or existential but also *social* freedom, a situation in which the son of an Italian laborer could learn to sing the blues. To wit, blues and spiritual are central black traditions that, though distinct from jazz, have revitalized and blackened the jazz tradition in the cities. Jazz – and this is of central importance – emerged in cities and developed with increasing distance from the cotton fields; it is therefore essentially a cultural product of the *city*. It flowered in cities where a great number of classes and cultures merged and meshed, cities that did not have an old cultural profile but were – like America itself – brand new and wide open. Jazz arose in this setting and its first name, *novelty music,* called attention to the slogan of Modernism: "Make it new." Modernism gave jazz its penchant for innovation; yet jazz, like many products of the new capitalism, could easily have ended in sterile commodification if it weren't for an irrepressible African element in it, a disruptive, antinomian vitality. Therefore we ought to expand the slogan "Make it new" and add "But not quite on the beat."[18] With Louis Armstrong in the twenties, jazz stopped being a collective folk music and became a Modernist art whose hallmarks were originality and innovation.

In a perpetual contest with his peers, the jazz musician must assert his individuality by enlarging the collective grammar of jazz expression. Learning from tradition by copying masters, the jazz artist's goal is to overcome his peers in the so-called cutting contests. The progress from copying to ironic quoting to critical travesty to reconstruction is one of increasing self-discipline. Characteristic of jazz are improvisation, open-ended innovation, and versatility, a constant negotiation between travesty, quotation, and masking and a perpetual making it new as a principle of composition as improvisation. It is dialogic, combative, antiphonal. And it connects with Eliot's "Tradition and the Individual Talent." Here is Ellison running jazz through Eliot's changes:

> For true jazz is an art of individual assertion within and against the group. Each true jazz moment (as distinct from the uninspired commercial performance) springs from a contest in which each artist challenges all the rest; each solo flight, or improvisation, represents (like the successive canvases of a painter) a definition of his identi-

ty: as individual, as member of the collectivity and as a link in the chain of tradition. (*SA*, 234)

The true jazz moment could be defined as ecstatic creativity in transience. The jazz session is an ephemeral happening in which creation, reception, composition, and performance become one. This explains why jazz was so attractive to the Modernist avant-garde in literature and art. The drive for innovation, which is so characteristic of jazz, identifies it as a truly Western child of Modernism. There is that discipline of making it new. Yet, jazz is not exclusively Western. The ritual and the nature of the jazz event owe a lot to an older, Afro-American, perhaps even African tradition. Whereas in Western music there is a division of labor between composer and musician, the jazz musician is both. Such performance requires a new creative spontaneity that Charles Mingus describes in the following manner:

> Each musician when he takes a horn in his hand – trumpet, bass, saxophone, drums – whatever instrument he plays – each soloist, that is, when he begins to ad lib on a given composition with a title and improvise a new creative melody, this man is taking the place of a composer. He is saying, "Listen, I am going to give you a new melodic conception on a tune you are familiar with. I am a composer." That's what he is saying. I, myself, came to enjoy the players who didn't only swing, but who invented new rhythmic patterns, along with new melodic concepts. And those people are: Art Tatum, Bud Powell, Max Roach, Sonny Rollins, Lester Young, Dizzy Gillespie and Charles Parker, who is the greatest genius of all to me because he changed the whole era around. But there is no need to compare composers. If you like Beethoven, Bach or Brahms, that's okay. They were all pencil composers. I always wanted to be a spontaneous composer.[19]

The performing composer radicalizes the act of composition. It is imperative that he innovate, and in a seemingly spontaneous fashion. The worst put-down of a jazz musician is that he repeats himself. The pianist Bill Evans writes:

> There is a Japanese visual art in which the artist is *forced* to be *spontaneous*. He must paint on a thin stretched parchment with a special brush and black water paint in such a way that an unnatural or interrupted stroke will destroy the line or break through the

113

parchment. Erasures or changes are impossible. These artists must practice a particular *discipline,* that of allowing the idea to express itself in communication with their hands in such a direct way that deliberation cannot interfere.

The resulting pictures lack the complex composition and texture of ordinary painting, but it is said that those who see well find something captured that escapes explanation.

This conviction that *direct deed* is the most meaningful reflection, I believe, has prompted the evolution of the extremely severe and unique *disciplines* of the jazz or improvising musician. Group improvisation is a further challenge. Aside from the weighty technical problem of collective coherent thinking, there is the very human, even *social* need for sympathy from all members to *bend for the common result.*[20]

The Modernist drive for innovation appears in song titles: "Things to Come," "Now's the Time," "Tempus Fugit." In short, the essence of jazz is a constant overcoming, a transcendence in art of the limitations of the status quo. Jazz lives in a perpetual opposition to existing systems of musical expression. Hence it expresses for Ellison the central drive and function of art. Protest, he argues, should not be the content but the essence of art "as technical assault against the styles which have gone before" (*SA,* 142).

The language of jazz is expressive of this deep desire. Those unwilling to swing through the changes are known as *squares, lames,* or *moldy figs* – all words expressing stasis and paralysis – whereas jazz musicians have referred to themselves as *hepcats, hipsters, swingers,* and so on. Even deeper are the terms for music itself: *jazz, boogie-woogie, rock 'n roll, jive* – all connoting movement and sexual activity. Dance and sex underlie these names. Linguists have traced the etymology of *jazz* as a creole word meaning to speed up, implying, inevitably, orgasm.[21] Radical critics have worried about this sexual mortgage of jazz. There has been many a Mr. Clean in black cultural nationalism who wanted to excise this libidinal aura of jazz. But there is no easy or ideological way out of history; jazz arose as an antirepressive freedom zone in a basically prohibitive society, a society that for a long stretch of its history was hostile to dance, song, sex. Jazz articulates those experiences that do not conform easily to ideology or to attempts at colonization. It is essentially anarchistic, though never undisciplined. This is one reason why jazz has not fared well in totalitarian systems:

Nazis *and* Stalinists rejected it violently. In fact, it is a sort of litmus test for exposing authoritarianism and fundamentalism, and therefore it comes as no surprise that not only the KGB but also American religious fundamentalists are united in their resolve to combat it, each of them calling it an invention of the enemy. Christian Crusade Publications of Tulsa, Oklahoma, has complained that jazz is part of a Communist master music plan;[22] conversely, Stalinists called it a form of capitalist depravity, and Nazis referred to it as degenerate art. The totalitarian international clearly did not like it for its liberating potential, its subtly subversive and seductive nature, and its antidogmatic stance.

Ellison called jazz "that embodiment of a superior democracy in which each individual cultivated his uniqueness and yet did not clash with his neighbors." Jazz is by no means democratic in the sense of being noncompetitive; however, its main goal is not just to cut the other player, but to cut him by conquering one's own limitations and by becoming better than before. Improvisation is not free in the sense of being arbitrary. It follows the difficult discipline of searching out the inherent curve of language as collective consciousness in finding the inherent rhythms and rituals of the vernacular. Neither free verse nor improvisation is free, but each is similar in that each overcomes staid limitations. Ellison mentions that he heard the sound of jazz in Eliot's *The Waste Land*, the flagship of Modernist poetry. Eliot did not forget the sounds of his home town, St. Louis, one of the most important thoroughfares of the sounds of the Mississippi. Note too that in *Sweeney Agonistes*, Eliot quotes "Under the Bamboo Tree," a composition by Bob Cole, the partner of Rosamond Johnson, whose brother, James Weldon Johnson, wrote the first major novel of black musicality, *The Autobiography of an Ex-Colored Man*. (In that keystone novel the driving passion of the *ex-colored* – and, in Ellison's term, *invisible* – protagonist was, for a time, to bring black music into the American mainstream.)

The politics of being Ellison[23]

There has been a good deal of politically inspired interpretation of Ellison's work. His rejoinder that he is an artist, not a party politician, has not silenced the ongoing discussion, which is cluttered up by questionable background assumptions. Briefly, then, let me review some of the controversies and speculate on their deeper motives.

For one who values improvisation, dialogue, and innovation, Ellison does not have much tolerance for black writers who use an unfinished or loosely improvisational style. Though aesthetically motivated, this rejection of a good deal of black writing may, and certainly has been, read politically. For Ellison much of the writing of Zora Neale Hurston or Langston Hughes, for example, is not good enough, not up to Modernist standards. His jester's love of folklore and of a freewheeling anthropology is disciplined by a high priest's Modernist values. Whereas folklore is his freedom, Modernism is his necessity. He urges a greater freedom in the discovery of a rich cultural heritage but curtails and domesticates it by his Modernist dictates. The contradiction extends to his political philosophy. Whereas his political ideal seems to tend toward an antihegemonic notion of grass-roots egalitarian democracy (i.e., the antinomian American tradition from Emerson to Whitman), his aesthetic choice of Modernism is tied to a hierarchical, even aristocratic, notion of cultural excellence. Modernism as a program implies an evolutionary fiction of poetic improvement; it sets in motion an unending spiral of maximizing poetic profit, a development that tends toward elitism, alienation, and isolation. These are indeed labels Ellison has learned to live with. His group anthropology battles (and perhaps loses) against an individualistic aesthetic. For Ellison, when the chips are down, individual talent beats tradition.

Behind this conflict lurk two notions of culture. One is egalitarian and free-wheeling, inspired by a black and general American vernacular tradition; the other is hierarchical and tight, beholden to a Western aristocracy of values. The division splits Ellison's kin: His relatives belong to the first, his ancestors to the second cultural definition.

This conflict is, of course, at the bottom of all discussions about the role of black intellectuals: whether to remain loyal to the group at the price of self-marginalization or to "whup the game" (and join it) at the price of losing one's group. Ellison cannot be accused of ignoring the problem; it is, in fact, his central theme. The unconvincing ending of "Flying Home" may be an indication that he doesn't have the answer. In the story the protagonist, Todd, is "reconciled" with the black folk. But perhaps Ellison is putting us on; who knows?

How can one square the circle of intellectual excellence and group loyalty, of individuation through art and loyalty to collective vernacular traditions, of effective group politics and cosmopolitanism? It has been argued that by lifting folklore out of the folk horizon and giving it the high seriousness of Modernism, Ellison has pulled its political teeth and robbed it of its antinomian power. Joel Chandler Harris turned the basically malevolent Brer Rabbit into a domestic pet. Did not Ellison turn the antinomianism of folklore into "celebration"? Even so, Ellison must be credited with giving the lore cultural power within the mainstream.

The fact that his Modernist aesthetic tends toward his own isolation and ultimate silence weighs more heavily. Modernism (and perhaps all great art) rejects the common reader and is punished by ever decreasing audiences and continued misunderstanding. On a very pragmatic level, therefore, the stern discipline of Modernism has tended to undo Ellison's liberating folk ethos or has given it the lie.

To this seemingly insoluble problem, jazz signals a political solution. Jazz indeed is a squaring of the circle: It is deeply rooted in the black folk and its music (Charlie Parker and Ornette Coleman played in jump bands), and it has repeatedly been revitalized by black folk energy, by blues and gospel. At the same time, it is a global Modernist idiom. It transcends or simply ignores ethnic boundaries, and that makes it suspect to all sorts of cultural nationalists. And it is a musical creole that is neither purely African nor purely Euro-American, yet is inconceivable without black participation in a key role. Whereas one could easily envisage the rise of jazz without the *Spanish tinge* (Jelly Roll Morton's phrase) or without the French input, it would be inconceivable without its African base. And what's more, jazz mediates a cultural contradiction: Though socially a subculture, it has been an aesthetic avant-garde since the time of Armstrong's Hot Five. Jazz, then, encapsulates best the contradictions that went into the making of a black-

117

inspired American culture. Its very existence and resilience are Ellison's proof of the pudding. Declared dead many times, like the contemporary novel it has ignored its obituaries. And it has made possible some of the highest achievements in American art. One needs to know these ramifications of the jazz phenomenon as part of a truly American vernacular in order to understand Ellison's deep commitment to jazz – not only as a form of music making but also as a paradigm for the manifold processes of historical give-and-take, of borrowing and exchanging, misunderstanding and misappropriation, but also of celebration. Jazz embodies, in its very substance, the complex fate and stern discipline of an American art. What indeed *would* America be like without blacks?

NOTES

1. There is a family resemblance in the philosophical outlooks of slipped Marxists. Though Ellison was never a member of the Marxist priesthood or a true believer, he participated in the Marxist spring of American letters, and he shared the disillusionment in "the God that failed." His antidogmatic stance resembles that of Leszek Kolakowski, who characterizes the antagonism between static and dynamic world views anthropomorphically: "The priest is the guardian of the absolute; he sustains the cult of the final and the obvious as acknowledged by and contained in tradition. The jester is he who moves in good society without belonging to it, and treats it with impertinence; he who doubts all that appears self-evident. He could not do this if he belonged to good society; he would then be at best a scandalmonger. The jester must stand outside good society and observe it from the sidelines in order to unveil the nonobvious behind the obvious, the nonfinal behind the final; yet he must frequent society so as to know what it holds sacred and to have the opportunity to address it impertinently." "The Priest and the Jester" in Kolakowski, *Toward a Marxist Humanism* (New York: Grove Press, 1968), pp. 33–4. The jester, of course, is kin to the trickster; cf. the following discussion.

2. Armstrong has been credited with a great number of pithy statements. This quote, which may well belong to oral legend, was taken from liner notes on Paquito D'Rivera's record *"Live at Keystone Korner."* Even if it isn't true, it is fitting. It is also interesting that this sort of statement should be eagerly picked up by transcultural artists such as

Paquito D'Rivera, who is a Cuban disciple of Charlie Parker, Ornette Coleman, and Earl Bostic all in one.

3. Ralph Ellison, *Shadow and Act* (New York: Random House, 1964), pp. 172–3. This volume will be cited hereafter as *SA*.

4. Ralph Ellison, "Remembering Richard Wright," *Delta* 18 (April 1984):7.

5. Kenneth Burke, *The Philosophy of Literary Form: Studies in Symbolic Action* (Baton Rouge: Louisiana State University Press, 1941; New York: Vintage Books, 1957), p. 16.

6. Ellison, *Going to the Territory* (New York: Random House, 1985), p. 300 (my emphasis). This volume will be cited hereafter as *GT*.

7. This term was coined by Kenneth Burke, and, like *double consciousness* (DuBois), has become a key word in ethnic cultural studies. Kenneth Burke, who is a philosophical maverick and not easy to read, is a magician with concepts. Philosophically speaking, Ellison drew his inspiration from *The Philosophy of Literary Form: Studies in Symbolic Action*, which may, with great profit, be read alongside *Shadow and Act*.

8. There is no indication that Ellison had intended to quote Martin Buber's philosophy of "I and thou"; yet there is sympathy for the Talmudic argument in his essays, which caused Irving Howe some dismay. Ellison links black and Jewish culture as being committed to the "word"; and Leslie Fiedler recognizes Ellison: "Oh, he's a black Jew."

9. The pervasiveness of signifying as a special type of black, perhaps African-derived, speech behavior was noted by folklorists and linguists: Roger Abrahams, *Deep Down in the Jungle: Negro Narrative Folklore from the Streets of Philadelphia* (Hatboro, Pa.: Folklore Associates, 1964). A black anthropological linguist, Claudia Mitchell-Kernan, picked up on Abraham's work and that of Thomas Kochman's "Toward an Ethnography of Black American Speech Behavior" in Norman E. Whitten and John F. Szwed, eds., *Afro-American Anthropology* (New York: The Free Press, 1979) and placed it in a black sociolinguistic context: "Signifying," in Alan Dundes, ed., *Mother Wit from the Laughing Barrel: Readings in the Interpretation of Afro-American Folklore* (Englewood Cliffs, N.J.: Prentice-Hall, 1973). The black poet Carolyn Rodgers used it to explain certain features of black poetry: "Black Poetry – Where It's At," *Negro Digest,* 18 (September 1969): 7–16, which again inspired my own article, "Contemporary Afro-American Culture: The Sixties and the Seventies," *Recherches Anglaises*

119

et Americaines (RANAM), Revue Annuelle, X (1977):131–53. Recently, signifying was discovered by the agenda setters of literary criticism as a *central* category to explain black culture and literature. If one were to look for just one strategy or frame of reference as a key to black culture (an operation that is in itself futile), then I would, with Ellison, rather opt for jazz, which, incidentally, involves a lot of signifying. Cf. Henry-Louis Gates, " 'The Blackness of Blackness': A Critique of the Sign and the Signifying Monkey," *Critical Inquiry*, 9 (June 1983):685–723.

10. Lawrence Levine, *Black Culture and Black Consciousness* (New York: Oxford University Press, 1977), pp. 405–6 (emphasis added).

11. Joseph Trimmer, ed., *A Casebook on Ralph Ellison's "Invisible Man"* (New York: Thomas Y. Crowell, 1972), p. 254.

12. Dena Epstein, "Myths About Black Folk Music," in William Ferris and Mary L. Hart, eds., *Folk Music and Modern Sound* (Oxford: University of Mississippi Press, 1982), p. 152.

13. Before him, Sterling Brown and Langston Hughes had discovered the latent creativity and hidden potential of the vernacular, but their art did not tackle or challenge contemporary Modernist forms. Ellison went one step further in forging a marriage between Modernist narrative techniques (making use of sophisticated notions of the narrative self and its many voices) and the black vernacular (with its pluralism of styles, rituals, and rhythms).

14. "Ralph Ellison Views Life and Literature," an interview with Hollie I. West, *The Washington Post*, August 19–21, 1973, p. 39.

15. Ralph Ellison, "A Very Stern Discipline," *Harper's Magazine* 234 (March 1967):84.

16. Robert B. Stepto, *From Behind the Veil: A Study of Afro-American Narrative* (Urbana: University of Illinois Press, 1979).

17. Amiri Baraka (Leroi Jones), *Black Music* (New York: William Morris, 1964), p. 155.

18. Simone Vauthier, " 'Not Quite on the Beat': An Academic Interpretation of the Narrative Stances in Ralph Ellison's *Invisible Man*," *Delta* 18 (April 1984):69–88.

19. Liner notes: Charles Mingus, "Let My Children Hear Music," Columbia K 31039.

20. Liner notes: Miles Davis, "Kind of Blue," Columbia CL 1355.

21. Cf. Irving Louis Horowits and Charles Nanry, "Ideologies and Theories about American Jazz," *Journal of Jazz Studies* 2 (June 1975):24–41.

22. David A. Noebel, *Rhythm, Riots and Revolution* (Tulsa: Christian

Crusade Publications, 1966), is firmly convinced that beat, rock 'n roll, and hot jazz are part of a communist master music plan. More about this topic in my "Bebop und die Beat Generation: Avantgarden oder Subkulturen?" *Amerikastudien/American Studies* 30, No. 4 (1985):509–35.

23. "All literature is political." In the first draft of this chapter, composed while I was still in Germany, I was going to let the issue of Ellison's politics rest right there. I assumed that Ellison's place in the literary pantheon was secure and his work above such quotidian concerns. I was wrong. Ellison continues to inspire controversies in America among both white and black critics. The discussion has progressed beyond the previous Ellison-versus-Wright-who-is-better-or-blacker stage, but he does not meet with the veneration here that he unquestionably enjoys in Europe. The following ruminations were inspired by lively discussions in the Afro-American Studies and W. E. B. DuBois colloquia at Harvard. My thanks are due to my hosts, Werner Sollors and Nathan Huggins, and to the DuBois Institute for a fellowship in the spring of 1986 that enabled me to complete this chapter.

5

Ellison's Masks and the Novel of Reality

THOMAS SCHAUB

For the first time, the stage scenery of the senses collapsed; the human mind felt itself stripped naked, vibrating in a void of shapeless energies. . . . Society became fantastic, a vision of Pantomime with a mechanical motion.
—Henry Adams, *The Education of Henry Adams*

I began this search for the real in a book called *Personae*, casting off, as it were, complete masks of the self in each poem. I continued in a long series of translations, which were but more elaborate masks.
—Ezra Pound, *Gaudier-Brzeska*

What! The world a gradual improvisation?
—George Santayana, *Winds of Doctrine*

1

ALTHOUGH *Invisible Man* appeared in 1952, Ralph Ellison's literary career had begun in 1937, at Richard Wright's firm insistence, with a review of Waters Turpin's novel *These Low Grounds* for the Communist-funded magazine *New Challenge*. In the period between 1937 and 1952, Ellison published nine short stories and dozens of essays and reviews.[1] Ellison's development during much of that time helps bring into full relief this transitional period in American fiction, for although his compass inscribed roughly the same arc that others' had, from economic determinism and class consciousness to private psychological interpretations of experience, Ellison's *Invisible Man* retains a broad political focus on both race consciousness and national culture by redefining the terms of social reality. ┤ for the black man

When Ralph Ellison accepted the National Book Award in

1953, he declared the "chief significance of *Invisible Man* as a fiction" to be its "experimental attitude, and its attempt to return to the mood of personal moral responsibility for democracy which typified the best of our nineteenth-century [American] fiction."[2] Though narrative experiment and social responsibility are inseparably linked in this statement, the novel's first admirers openly praised *Invisible Man* for going beyond social realism and the protest novel. R. W. B. Lewis, for example, noted (with favor) the novel's contentment with "its own being" and the absence of any impulse within it "to atone for some truculence in nature or to affect the course of tomorrow's politics."[3] Predictably, the novel was (and continues to be) attacked from the left for the very same reasons.[4] Ellison seems to have been willing to go along with his admirers' view of *Invisible Man,* and his collection of essays, *Shadow and Act* (1964), at many points confirms the priority of art over politics that many readers have attributed to him.

Yet political and social leadership were very much on Ellison's mind during the composition of *Invisible Man.* "This was the late forties," he told one interviewer, "and I kept trying to account for the fact that when the chips were down, Negro leaders did not represent the Negro community" (*SA*, 18). To find models of leadership, Ellison turned back to the nineteenth century, not only to Emerson and Melville but to the political figures of Frederick Douglass and W. E. B. Dubois, both of whom became presiding spirits of his novel. As we shall see, the vision of social reality in *Invisible Man* upon which so much critical attention has been centered makes little sense without the "experimental attitude" many critics have thought apolitical. For the novel's democratic authority — its capacity to speak to our culture — derives precisely from its insistent disclaimer of any reality other than its own life "as a fiction."

At the time Ellison was writing *Invisible Man,* many thought that the authority of a novel depends, as Philip Rahv wrote in 1942, upon "the principle of realism," which had taught writers "how to grasp and encompass the ordinary facts of human existence." In Rahv's view, the novelist's "medium knows of no other principle of coherence."[5] Lionel Trilling seconded this conviction in his influential essay "Morals, Manners, and the Novel," where he defined the novel as "a perpetual quest for reality, the field of its research being always manners as the indication of the direction of man's soul."[6] Both Rahv and Trilling looked to nineteenth-century European realism for their model of what the novel should be, and both men regarded Henry James's work as the only American fiction to approach that standard.

The problem – as Ellison analyzed it during the years he worked on his novel – was that the "forms of so many works" that had impressed him were "too restricted to contain the experience" that he knew (*SA*, 103). Twentieth-century American fiction, in particular, was inadequate to the "diversity of American life" generally, and had shown itself especially inept (and irresponsible) in portraying the realities of black life, which, Ellison argued, had been largely absent from American realist and naturalist fiction. "When the white American," Ellison wrote in 1946, "holding up most twentieth-century fiction, says, 'This is American reality,' the Negro tends to answer . . . 'Perhaps, but you've left out this, and this, and this. And most of all, what you'd have the world accept as *me* isn't even human'" (*SA*, 25).

As for Trilling's prescriptions, Ellison answered them directly in an essay published in 1955 titled "Society, Morality, and the Novel": "thank God again that the nineteenth century European novel of manners is dead, for it has little value in dealing with our world of chaos and catastrophe."[7] The reality Ellison sought to convey couldn't be "caught for more than the briefest instant in the tight well-made Jamesian novel, which was, for all its artistic perfection, too concerned with 'good taste' and stable areas." Nor did the forms of the more recent "hard-boiled" novel offer him a model, for its "hard-boiled stance and its monosyllabic utterance" were "embarrassingly austere" when set beside the "rich babel of idiomatic expression around me, a language full of imagery and gesture and rhetorical canniness" (*SA*, 103).

In many respects, *Invisible Man* may be understood less as a repudiation of such forms than as an improvisation upon them. After all, the novel begins with what appears to be a material and social definition of identity: "I am a man of substance, of flesh and bone," invisible only "because people refuse to see me" (3). In the ironic connotations that radiate from the word *substance*, Ellison playfully alludes to the novel of manners, and the black vet's advice to Invisible Man, "for God's sake, learn to look beneath the surface" (151), is not only the advice of a realist but perhaps an echo of James's exhortation to the novice writer "to be one of those people on whom nothing is lost!" Initially, everything is lost upon Invisible Man, as he tells us, and it is some time before he acquires what James called the *penetrating imagination* that allows him to interpret the manners of the society that both enslaves and excludes him.

Though this imagination was slow to develop in *Invisible Man*, his story, spoken to us from the bright darkness of his subterranean cell, is proof of his growth and of his "transformation" – as Ellison wrote later of his character – "from ranter to writer" (*SA*, 57). Invisible Man comes to see that he lives in a world whose manners obey a collective and distorting psychology that avoids acknowledging, often wilfully, what runs the social reality in which he moves. Without this understanding, Invisible Man is exiled to a land of surfaces in which he earnestly speaks his part in a social play he thinks is real. The irony of that participation pervades the medium and tone of Invisible Man's autobiography as he submits his earlier selves to his present scrutiny and shares in the reader's astonishment that so late in the game he was still asking: "what on earth was hiding behind the face of things?" (482).

But the radical consequences that follow from taking the black doctor's advice seriously propel both the novel and its speaker far beyond those narrative forms that Ellison specified. For although Ellison has described his novel as one about "innocence and human error, a struggle through illusion to reality" (*SA*, 117), the "reality" Invisible Man finds when he looks "beneath the surface" is not the objective "common ground" that the "principle of realism" is thought to uncover. When Invisible Man looks behind the face of things, he discovers chaos, an absence of any absolute meaning or pattern or "substance." His education is progressively radical, one that continues even as he tells his story, for though it begins with a naturalistic revelation of social manipulation, it evolves in the Rinehart chapter to a suspicion that identity is only

126

a mask, that "truth [is] always a lie," and that all action may be "betrayal" (482, 487, 495).

Social reality and its manners can be shown to operate by discernible forces, but they have no necessary substance outside the social theater that embodies them in a self-perpetuating fiction. Society becomes for Invisible Man, as it did for Henry Adams, "fantastic, a vision of Pantomime with a mechanical motion." For Ellison, the words *society* or *social reality* did not refer – as Rahv, Trilling, Howe, and other contemporaries implied they did – to an external world that the novel might mirror or picture, but rather to some idea of the world. Ellison knew, as Santayana had written in his essay "The Genteel Tradition," that "ideas are not mirrors, they are weapons" and that society operates by the ideology of its self-image.[8]

The paralyzing feature of this pantomime, however, is that so few of its company, rarely those who write the parts, are aware of the illusion they think is real. Invisible Man is in a unique position to see through this "reality" precisely because he has been excluded from it or may participate in it only on the condition that he remain invisible. This is the unique vantage point of both the protagonist, as a black man, and Ellison himself, as a black writer determined to make room on the stage for his own fiction, and in so doing to help renew in American society a more experimental and democratic attitude. At the same time, one of Ellison's challenges in writing his novel was not only to expose this exclusive reality but to do so without supplying in its place another fiction, equally monolithic.

To achieve this, Ellison had to invent a narrative form that would emerge from within and confirm the insights of his major character. Ellison's invention of a form that would confirm the authority of his vision coincides (within the narrative) with Invisible Man's evolving sense of his own form and the true basis of any power he possesses. The book begins at an indeterminate point in this evolution when Invisible Man, employing a dialectic bordering on self-contradiction, claims invisibility to be his form. Though this amounts to an acceptance of the fact that to others in society he is invisible, this acceptance involves a recognition of himself and his true social standing – a self-consciousness figured in the 1,369 lights that line his retreat and provide him with a form: "Without light I am not only invisible, but formless as well; and to be unaware of one's form is to live a death. I myself, after existing some twenty years, did not become alive until I discovered my invisibility" (7).[9]

This "darkness visible" is also the form of the novel itself, which employs oxymoron as a governing method by which the reader is immersed in the same contradictions that plague Invisible Man. Readers are asked repeatedly to entertain such apparent contradictions as the black hole that is brighter than Broadway, the "dream world" that is "only too real," and the "music of invisibility" that is visibly before us on the printed page. For Ellison (writing in 1946), it was just this intrinsic "ambivalence" of "the word" – its ability to mean opposite things at the same time – that made it the ideal medium for conveying "the full, complex ambiguity of the human" (*SA*, 25). It also helped him solve the problem of exposing one ideology without supplying another – at least another of the same kind. For although the idea that human existence is intrinsically ambiguous is itself an ideology, Ellison used it as a self-limiting device so that any articulated vision would always be inherently modest, aware of itself as a necessary fiction.

Such contradiction becomes the most faithful representation of human circumstances, for there is complete congruence here between the perception of an insubstantial reality and the adoption of an interior mode of expression that gives form (in its very syntax and vocabulary) to the absence of form. This is merely to state the obvious: Having struck through the social mask and found a cosmic charade in process, Invisible Man loses even the illusion of his bodily substance and is left only with his invisible, psychological reality. From this vantage point, *Invisible Man* tells its story from the inside out, so that "reality" is not merely "out there" to be found lurking among visible signs, but within the perception that constitutes – for each person – the relation of self and world. Here Invisible Man and *Invisible Man* coincide, as the book's words and its hero's "disembodied voice" stand as the only reality presented to the reader.

For the better part of the novel, Invisible Man appears to struggle with two ideas of reality: one that portrays a solid social world in which he wishes to play a part, and one that renders the depth of that social world as mere surface, in which no action short of charlatanism seems possible. In both ideas, however, reality remains merely external, and it is this epistemological naiveté that Invisible Man must outgrow. This naiveté is in part the understandable result of the protagonist's exclusion from society, but in Ellison's vision his character can fit himself for that social reality only by first coming to terms with the chaotic fluidity of existence itself. This decision was part of Ellison's effort to locate some ground of commonality outside the conventional terms of social discourse (of visible class and race), which tended only to perpetuate the absence of such community. Ellison thus twists his novel in a spiraling curve that elevates his character above and outside the theater he took to be real, until – having traveled through the ether of absurdity – he rediscovers the justification of social diversity and unity, and is thus in a position to suggest a more ambivalent (and benign) social order.

As a novel of social exclusion, *Invisible Man* describes a culture in which the difference that separates black from white, both within society and within the mind that has internalized those symbolic pigments, is a difference of race so vast that Invisible Man is not merely awkward or out of place. He is invisible. Though this condition of being excluded is one that Ellison universalizes, it has its origin in race relations and is the initial and unproblematic meaning of the psychological reality Ellison sought to represent: "you often doubt if you really exist. You wonder whether you aren't simply a phantom in other people's minds. . . . You ache with the need to convince yourself that you do exist in the real world" (*IM*, 3–4). In "Harlem Is Nowhere" (1948), Ellison described the effort of a psychiatric clinic in Harlem to ameliorate the psychopathology of blacks who had "no stable, recognized place in society." Sometimes their feeling of being "nowhere" erupts in mass riots – Ellison cites the Harlem riots of 1935 and 1943 – but this seething explosiveness has been ignored because "there is an argument in progress between black men and white men as to the true nature of American reality" (*SA*, 300, 301).

Ellison's adoption of narrative modes that depart from the conventions of realism and manners thus has a political motive: His use of interior, psychological forms is an effort to take part in that ongoing argument by presenting the reality of the "sense of unreality that haunts Harlem" (*SA*, 302). Ellison's novelistic aim is to identify and dramatize the medium that embraces the opposing voices of American culture, and by so doing to remind readers of the dream of freedom and diversity that has informed the culture from its inception. His strategy is to make Invisible Man's sense of unreality the ticket of admission to the very society that has rejected him by showing the condition of exclusion to be the universal human experience.

An indivisible element of that project is Ellison's own assertion, which the entire novel enacts, of belonging to a particular tradition of American literature. The speaker's first words ("I am an invisible man") are an act of self-definition meant to evoke the beginnings of *Walden, Moby-Dick,* and *Huckleberry Finn.* Each of these narratives establishes the self – temporarily in retreat, on pond, sea, or river – as the origin of discussions concerning the relations of self and society, and each parlays the apparent directness of colloquial speech into the opportunity to elaborate upon the more indirect and complex nature of those relations. The invocation of Poe ("No, I am not a spook like those who haunted Edgar Allan Poe"), although distinguishing the narrator's being from mere phantasm, employs not a little irony in the deadpan use of racist idiom and alludes to the tradition of nightmare and symbolic landscape in which *Invisible Man* also claims a place. In the great exuberance with which Ellison makes use of these (and many other) narrative traditions, he was flaunting the power of language to provide him a place within those traditions; at the same time, the high visibility of his allusions established his conscious control over and distance from them.[10]

The narrator, of course, goes to great lengths to declare his Americanness by locating himself in "the great American tradition of tinkers. That makes me kin to Ford, Edison and Franklin" (7). A tinker, it should be remembered, is not only a mender but an unskillful and itinerant one as well, one whose attempts at tinkering often prove fruitless. There is implicit in Ellison's comic play on the ambiguities of this word an entire theory of American culture and history as the ongoing patching of a persistent rent, like that of the Joads' automobile carrying them West. This schism is given some specificity in the hero's use of electricity to light his cell, for, like Franklin, Invisible Man has learned to take the power of the heavens for his own use; but here the electricity comes not from the sky but from those false white gods of commerce who profit from Monopolated Light & Power (7). Invisible Man is thus also a comic Prometheus who has stolen the fire with which the gods had burned him on the electric carpet of the battle royal (27).

Because the light that this power makes possible is then used by Ellison as a metaphor of the self-consciousness and awareness that give Invisible Man his form and life, we may see how extraordinarily Ellison has patched together the implications of his metaphors. One metaphor literally depends upon the other, for to the degree that it must first be plugged in, Invisible Man's awareness is not entirely self-originating. Because the metaphor (lights = self-consciousness) works only if the power is turned on, his self-awareness is not merely the result of his criminal theft (free, private) but also a consequence of there being a public power to draw upon, a past and a society with which he can tinker. And this was as true for his author (Ellison) as it is for Invisible Man.

As a tinker, Invisible Man lives between the social factions he would mend: "I don't live in Harlem but in a border area. . . . I live rent-free in a building rented strictly to whites, in a section of the basement that was shut off and forgotten during the nineteenth century" (5). This "border area" to which Invisible Man has retreated is a kind of surreal Grasmere or Walden, and is part of the symbolic territory he shares with other occupants of the border in American literature. For Natty Bumppo, Hester Prynne, Ishmael, Huck Finn, and Lambert Strether, this territory helps define their relation between civilization and wilderness, past and future, order and chaos, fact and imagination, Europe and the New World. In the more recent literary past, Ellison's border area is meant to echo and revise the symbolic geography of Richard Wright's *Native Son* and the racial dualisms it charts between North and South, white and black, thought and emotion. Like Wright's map of the Dalton house, this border area not only describes a house divided against itself but also alludes to the history of this division. His hero is thus an underground man, meant to be associated with Dostoievski's character, living in that nether world of symbols whose literal and human embodiment is denied by what Pynchon, fourteen years later, would call the "cheered land."

Ellison's explicit use of symbolic space as the ground of reconciliation also recognizes the power of symbols to displace and repress the human realities with which they are correlated, for "if the word has the potency to revive and make us free, it has also the power to blind, imprison and destroy" (*SA*, 24). This negative power is part of the meaning impacted in the fact that the border area is not only a place but a time as well, "shut off and forgotten during the nineteenth century." Before the time of Reconstruction, the use of the black to symbolize humanity, Ellison argues, is "organic to nineteenth-century literature" and "occurs not only in Twain, but in Emerson, Thoreau, Whitman and Melville" (*SA*, 32). The black had begun to "exert an influence upon America's moral consciousness" and "during the nineteenth century it flared nakedly in the American consciousness, only to be repressed after the Reconstruction" (*SA*, 29). Instead, the black becomes in twentieth-century fiction "an image of the unorganized, irrational forces of American life" (*SA*, 41). By comparison with "this continuing debasement of our image," Ellison declares in another essay, "the indignities of slavery were benign" (*SA*, 48).

When Ellison began to write *Invisible Man* in 1945, Brown v. Board of Education (1954) was still nine years in the future and the "separate but equal" doctrine of Plessy v. Ferguson (1896) still obtained. When Invisible Man reflects upon the false promise of manumission, however, he alludes not only to that doctrine but to the speech of Booker T. Washington's that anticipated its language, the Atlanta Compromise (1895): "About eighty-five years ago they were told that they were free, united with others of our country in everything pertaining to the common good, and, in everything social, separate like the fingers of the hand. And they believed it" (*IM*, 15)[11] The number of years refers to the date of Lincoln's Emancipation Proclamation (1862), but the words are Washington's (1895), and they prefigure Invisible Man's own willing complicity in what enslaves him. Ellison refers to both dates simultaneously to bracket that time (Reconstruction) when the moral role blacks had occupied in American culture was "shut off and forgotten," not only because blacks were "shackled to almost everything [the white folk mind] would repress from conscience and consciousness" (*SA*, 48) but because under Washington's leadership they acceded – in DuBois's word – to such "submission."

The novel speaks to us from this forgotten region, given life in the space-time of the hero's psychology, whose dimensions are at once those of his border area and of the novel itself. The novel's voice, that is, issues not only from a character but from a time and a place. By building these associations (with an earlier literature and politics) into the description of his hero's hideout, Ellison, too, is burrowing within the accepted order of the literary world. Like the "yokel" whose one blow knocks cold the "scientific" prize-fighter, Ellison steps "inside his opponent's sense of time." Because Invisible Man's references to himself as a tinkerer and a yokel express Ellison's idea of America as a do-it-yourself culture, they are always comic (and calculated) refractions of Ellison's self-image. The yokel's maneuver is Invisible Man's analogy for the effect of a reefer, which allowed him to hear the "unheard sounds" (which are sweeter) and to listen "not only in time, but in space as well" (8), but the novel itself is a kind of one-punch knockout that moves the reader about in both space and time.

Ellison's declared affinity for the moral ambiguities of nineteenth-century literature is part and parcel of his rejection of the dominant naturalistic prose of the twentieth century and the scientific assumptions on which it is based. Although "our naturalistic prose," Ellison wrote in 1946, is "perhaps the brightest instrument for recording sociological fact, physical action, the nuance of speech," it becomes "dull when confronting the Negro" (*SA*, 26). For Ellison, the rise of naturalism, with its emphasis upon the crushing influence of the environment, is a literary corollary of the growing influence of "contemporary science and industry," which has obscured the "full, complex ambiguity of the human" (*SA*, 25). Ellison's rejection is a shift in emphasis that declines the role of victim and recognizes the self as a participant in the creation of social reality.

In Ellison's thinking, Richard Wright's *Native Son* had reinforced

133

the image of the black man as a victim, and since it was written by a black man about a black figure, it helped to demonstrate the shortcomings of the naturalist method. Ellison had begun to write under Wright's prompting, and continued to write for *New Masses* from 1938 to 1942. The book reviews and articles he wrote during this period emphasize the economic basis of personality and social history,[12] but when he came to write his own fiction, he felt that Wright's interpretation of black experience had been too sociological, and that his character Bigger Thomas possessed none of the consciousness or imagination that Wright had in large measure: "I felt that Wright was overcommitted to ideology – even though I, too, wanted many of the same things for our people. You might say that I was much less a social determinist" (*SA*, 16).

Ellison thought that the limitations of Bigger Thomas were in part a consequence of the narrative form Wright elected to use, for the naturalist mode, like the wrong channel, simply bypassed other frequencies of being, to which he wanted to give air time. In "Twentieth-Century Fiction and the Black Mask of Humanity" (1946), Ellison associated "naturalistic prose" with exterior detail – "sociological fact, physical action, the nuance of speech." Thus he felt that it was disposed to offer only "counterfeit" images of the black man's humanity, which was hidden by the black mask and its stereotypical associations in the white mind. Because black humanity and its problems with white America are "psychological," an adequate image of the black man can emerge only from interior modes of expression (*SA*, 26–7). Wright's image of Bigger Thomas only confirmed "what whites think of the Negro's reality," he wrote in "The World and the Jug" (1964). "Here environment is all – and interestingly enough, environment conceived solely in terms of the physical, the non-conscious" (*SA*, 114).

Though the complexity and power of Wright's novel belie his view, Wright saw himself as Zola had described the novelist: "Why should I not, like a scientist in a laboratory, use my imagination and invent test-tube situations, place Bigger in them, and, following the guidance of my own hopes and fears . . . work out in fictional form an emotional statement and resolution of this problem?" Bigger is an "organism" who is "conditioned" by his environment, and who ends by "accepting what life had made him."[13]

Because Ellison felt that Wright's scientific attitude didn't allow for ways in which the individual might deviate from the generalizations and group comparisons of sociology and economic determinism, *Invisible Man* is full of parodies of scientific confidence. One example is the hospital scene in which Invisible Man undergoes shock treatment. Not yet a gadgeteer himself, he is still subject to the "little gadget[s]" of others; resting inside a glass box, wires attached to his head and navel in a mechanistic parody of fetal life, Invisible Man overhears the conversation of the doctors above him:

> "The machine will produce the results of a prefrontal lobotomy without the negative side effects of the knife," the voice said. . . .
> "But what of his psychology?"
> "Absolutely of no importance!" the voice said. "The patient will live as he has to live, and with absolute integrity. Who could ask for more? He'll experience no major conflict of motives, and what is even better, society will suffer no traumata on his account." (231)

Reflecting upon this experience, Invisible Man recalls that "some of it sounded like a discussion of history" (231). This scene thus satirizes Marxism as well as science, medicine, and industry, and anticipates the next major section of the novel, where Ellison's hero is told by the Brotherhood, "We are all realists here, and materialists"; "We follow the laws of reality" (300, 491).

This dialogue also sets forth the novel's opposition between the confidence in description that is often characteristic of the realist and the freedom of psychological reality to evade such description. Written in the late forties, the passage helps to show how realism, by becoming allied with a materialist view of human behavior, had lost its authority. Implicitly, Ellison's novel proposes a psychological narrative form — at places surreal and expressionistic — as being more realistic than the naturalism it supplants.

All of the foregoing — the desire for recognition, the assertion of Americanness, the novel's historical references, and Ellison's reasons for rejecting naturalism — makes sense in any view of the novel's commitment to social reality. No serious response to *Invisible Man* has failed to note this commitment, or to take into account its power as social indictment, but readers have neglected the way in which Ellison's authority to register such an indictment relies upon the novel's evolving experiment in narrative form.

The need for such experiment is already implicit in Ellison's view of the inadequacies of realism and naturalism, but there are further reasons that have to do with the "fantastic" world the hero eventually discovers. In making this discovery, he demonstrates how far he has come in taking the black doctor's advice to "look beneath the surface." But even more disquieting than the realization of the charade society has exerted to "Keep this Nigger-Boy Running" is the suspicion that the world to which he seeks admittance is *only* a charade. That suspicion, too, undermines the trustworthiness of realist picturing as a communal medium of candor, and this – along with his own invisibility – underlies his decision (and Ellison's) to substitute the word-as-sound (the "music of invisibility") for the word-as-picture, to trade being seen for being heard. For though Invisible Man begins his story by declaring himself to be "a man of substance" (3), he is by novel's end "without substance, a disembodied voice" (568).

2

To define Invisible Man's experience as an education in looking beneath the surface is, paradoxically, to frame the novel within the characteristic claim of realism, one of the forms that Ellison was at pains to amend and abridge. Within the abstract generality of this claim – to expose the way things really are – *Invisible Man* may be termed *realistic,* for it attempts to offer an expression adequate to the experience of living. But this realistic quality is achieved in the novel with techniques – not only of symbolic and surrealist presentation, but of self-conscious form – that violate the habitual decorum of realist conventions, especially as they were understood by the critic and writer in the forties.

The central device by which Ellison educates his character to the self-consciousness that defines the novel's reality is the image and idea of the mask. Images of the mask cluster about the intimations of political and sexual power, and, like words themselves, are a source of ambiguity revealing as much about their interpreter as

136

about the realities they appear to conceal. As we shall see, in fact, the masking and unmasking in which Invisible Man participates parallels the mask of language that constitutes his world. This paralleling is a political element in the novel because the inherent ambivalences of language have calcified – in the society to which Ellison was addressing his fiction – into a system of associations that excluded and imprisoned black reality within white stereotypes. Thus it was Ellison's strategy to submit not only Invisible Man, but the author and his reader as well, to the discipline of the mask.

When Invisible Man remembers himself standing before the statue of the college founder, whose hands are "outstretched in the breathtaking gesture of lifting a veil," he cannot "decide whether the veil is really being lifted, or lowered more firmly into place; whether [he is] witnessing a revelation or a more efficient blinding" (36). Clearly, the ambiguous gesture is fatal ("breathtaking") as well as awe-inspiring, for Ellison's use of the "veil" alludes to DuBois's attack on Booker T. Washington and reappears throughout *Invisible Man* as an image of false revelation.[14] One of the most compelling lures of the Brotherhood is its promise of powerful insight: "I had the sense of being present at the creation of important events, as though a curtain had been parted and I was being allowed to glimpse how the country operated" (298). This promise helps sustain the hero's naiveté even when he is demoted to lecturing on "The Woman Question": "Now was certainly no time for inactivity; . . . not at a time when all the secrets of power and authority still shrouded from me in mystery appeared on the way toward revelation" (397).[15]

Like all the other falls Invisible Man suffers in the novel, this one is fortunate and helps propel him toward the realization of the "lie that success is a rising *upward*" (498). Moreover, by means of this demotion, Ellison moves his novel toward the final but ironic union of power and sex when Invisible Man attempts to seduce prophecy from Sybil, a wife of one of the Brotherhood.

Ellison begins the orchestration of that union in Chapter 1 of the novel, where Invisible Man is forced to watch a nude dancer, whose "hair was yellow like that of a circus kewpie doll" and whose face was "heavily powdered and rouged, as though to form an abstract mask." She excites opposing emotions in the young hero ("I wanted . . . to caress her and destroy her, to love her and murder her"), and these emotions are matched by opposing similes; for her "kewpie doll" aspect competes with another interpretation that occurs to Invisible Man: "she seemed like a fair bird-girl girdled in veils calling to me from the angry surface of some gray and threatening sea" (19). The dancer herself remains invisible, hidden not only by the "abstract mask" of her makeup but by Invisible Man's images of her, which vacillate between circus doll and Botticelli's Venus.

The figure of the veiled alluring white woman recurs again and again in *Invisible Man*, but the symbolic associations that encircle her figure – so that it arouses both desire and guilt – are firmly established by Ellison's use of the character Mr. Norton. Norton, the white philanthropist and trustee of Invisible Man's college, is not merely a veiled allusion to Charles Eliot Norton and to white trustees everywhere, but is also a figure for the liberal, governed by too simple an idea of control, and whose good intentions disguise – especially from themselves – the persistence of racist assumptions. This view of liberal intentions was the substance of Ellison's fiery response to Irving Howe: "Many of those who write of Negro life today seem to assume that as long as their hearts are in the right place they can be as arbitrary as they wish in their formulations. . . . They write as though Negro life exists only in light of their belated regard" (*SA*, 123).

To Norton, his daughter was "a being more rare, more beautiful, purer, more perfect and more delicate than the wildest dream of a poet," and her death – which thwarted the best that "medical science" could do for her – has driven him to his "first-hand organizing of human life," to reaffirm the order threatened by the chaos of death. His daughter is the immaculate vision that holds up the entire edifice of civilization, so it is no wonder that the white woman, bearing these associations, should inspire both love and hatred in the black hero, whose pigmentation makes him the figure of chaos. With comic irony directed at both of the men in the car, Ellison alludes to the parallel between the garish dancer and Norton's sacred girl when Invisible Man thinks, "I seemed to remember her, or someone like her, in the past. I know now that it was the flowing costume of soft, flimsy material that made for the effect" (42).

That these associations are internal, psychological realities and compulsions is reinforced by their recurrence in Trueblood's dream, which follows closely upon the exchange within the car. In the sexual dream that results in an incestuous reality, Trueblood finds himself in a woman's room: "I looks over in a corner and sees one of them tall, grandfather clocks and I hears it strikin' and the glass door is openin' and a white lady is steppin' out of it. She got on a nightgown of soft white silky stuff and nothin' else, and she looks straight at me" (57). The clock is the appropriate symbol of Western order violated by Trueblood's presence, and appears in his dream because, while drifting off to sleep, he has "heard the clock up there at the school strikin' four times" (54). The clock makes the students – "uniforms pressed" and "minds laced up" – march to the time it imposes, and the white woman's presence at its center makes explicit the sexual repression that enforces the beat.

Trueblood, as his name implies, lives by his own tempo and tells his own story; for his dream images graphically depict the displaced and incestuous eros implicit in Norton's adulation of his daughter: "At first I couldn't git the door open, it had some kinda crinkly stuff like steel wool on the facing. But I gits it open and gits inside and it's hot and dark in there. I goes up a dark tunnel, up near where the machinery is making all that noise and heat. It's like the power plant they got up to the school" (58).

Trueblood is willing to take responsibility for the incest in which this dream culminates ("I makes up my mind that I ain't nobody but myself") and returns to face his wife and daughter, but both Norton and Invisible Man are horrified by his story. Invisible Man is worried that Trueblood will reflect negatively upon himself and the school, but underlying that fear is the one he shares with Norton: that reality and dream are not distinct realms after all, and that the dream of controlling reality is one for which – as the hero has learned by the time he writes the Prologue – "all dreamers and sleepwalkers must pay the price" (14). Invisible Man remains a sleepwalker for the greater part of the novel not only because his determination to be seen merely confirms the distorted image others have of him, but because his own vision is distorted by the same symbolic psychology that prevents others from seeing him.

Trueblood's self-reliance and his mesmerizing storytelling ability are inseparable elements of his unified being and differentiate him from both the white Trustee and his black sycophant. The larger significance of this integrated being will not become apparent to Invisible Man for many pages, yet it is the key to Ellison's sophisticated handling of structure and language in this novel, as well as the answer to Invisible Man's search for pattern and meaning.

Ellison is willing to suggest that such pattern exists, but only within experience, not in the reification of a symbolic world supposed to exist beyond or behind experience. Thus, when Invisible Man travels North from school, Ellison purposely floods the description of his departure with every literary, mythic, and symbolic trope he can muster:

> In less than five minutes the spot of earth which I identified with the best of all possible worlds was gone, lost within the wild uncultivated countryside. . . . I saw a moccasin wiggle swiftly along the gray concrete, vanishing into a length of pipe that lay beside the road. I watched the flashing past of cotton fields and cabins, feeling that I was moving into the unknown. (154)

Ellison exploits these echoes of literary and mythic understandings of human experience not only to emphasize that Invisible Man is recalling his feelings as the maudlin reflections of an earlier self – since this "spot of earth," earlier identified explicitly as "Eden" (109), is no more known to him than the metropolis he is about to enter – but also to call attention to the fictive structures by which we interpret our experience. This is the kind of doubleback joke that runs throughout the entire novel – as when Invisible Man feels a "sudden fit of blind terror" at being blindfolded: "I was unused to darkness," he says (121) – and that the novel itself as a self-conscious fiction enacts.

Thus, much of the novel's overt symbolic texture is not only an expression of the hero's present understanding being exercised at his own expense, but is doubly exploited by Ellison to dramatize the ambivalence of the word and its power to subordinate experience to symbolic correlative. The high visibility of the novel's symbolic texture should alert us to the amused distance that Ellison keeps from his own story, which, like Trueblood, he has learned to tell so well. Control comes from power over language, but this power defeats itself unless it is employed with knowledge of the distance that always exists between ideas and experience. In such passages as the preceding one, Ellison is not merely inverting white tropes, drawn from Milton and Voltaire; he is exploiting them *as* tropes, converting them into self-conscious, ironic fictions. Among the commentators of the time, Richard Chase alone nearly stumbled upon this comic irony informing Ellison's use of language: "most of his errors are, one might almost say, gratifyingly amateurish and gross. . . . There is something positively engaging in the fact that he calls two of his northern white gentlemen Mr. Emerson and Mr. Norton."[16]

Such comic distance always qualifies, for example, Ellison's use of myth to structure his novel, for the ultimate use of that structure is to return the hero to the embodiment of myth in experience. "I knew that in both *The Waste Land* and *Ulysses*," Ellison said in *The Paris Review* interview, "ancient myth and ritual were used to give form and significance to the material; but it took me a few years to realize that the myths and rites which we find functioning in our everyday lives could be used in the same way" (*SA*, 174). Ellison's use of these materials doesn't point toward a transcendent order of art or religion, but down to the "abiding patterns of experience which . . . help to form our sense of reality and from which emerge our sense of humanity and our conception of human value."[17] From Ellison's point of view, Eliot had replaced one narrative with another, but Ellison was trying to tell a story that would convey the reality of black life without at the same time appearing to fix the nature of reality or limit its permutations. Such a narrative would have to be, in some sense, an antinarrative, just as the visible form of its speaker is his invisibility.

Mythic order in *Invisible Man* always remains subordinate to the uses that it may have, just as narrative never acquires a reality beyond its purpose, both private and social, as a means of self-definition and renewal. In these terms, Invisible Man may be seen as a man determined to locate the material solidity of the narratives that entangle him; as a result of this naiveté, he remains divorced from experience and continues to think of the veils, curtains, and gowns of the novel as surfaces outside himself that — once parted — will reveal the reality and power he seeks.

We can measure how little Invisible Man has advanced by his reaction to the next incarnation of the white woman who haunts his waking nightmare. After his first lecture on "The Woman Question," one of the Brotherhood's wives seduces him, provoking in him the same ambivalent reactions that the blonde nude had inspired four hundred pages earlier: "I wanted both to smash her and to stay with her and knew that I should do neither." When he demands "What kind of game is this?", she expresses the reader's own amazement: "Oh, you poor darling! It isn't a game, really you have no cause to worry, we're free" (405).

Here, too, the vocabulary embodies the ambivalence and contradiction that are the governing principles of the novel's expression, for although the woman's invitation is not a game (nor are they free), Invisible Man's acceptance of it would be a large step toward learning how to "play the game." This latter contest is the game the black doctor refers to when counseling our hero (151), but Invisible Man cannot play along because he is unwilling to discard his superficial narrative of how things operate: "my mind whirled with forgotten stories of male servants summoned to wash the mistress's back. . . . Pullman porters invited into the drawing room of rich wives headed for Reno — thinking, But this is the movement, the Brotherhood" (406).

This mental struggle is reflected in the two mirrors that frame him and that "now like a surge of the sea tossed our images back and forth, back and forth." Here in the bedroom there is a battle taking place to define the nature of reality, but it is a curious and inherent feature of this battle that the opponents remain invisible to one another. In the midst of these reflections, Invisible Man sees the woman's "one free hand [go] up as though to smooth her hair and in one swift motion the red robe swept aside like a veil, and I went breathless at the petite and generously curved nude, framed delicate and firm in the glass." In the world of the novel, dream has become reality as Trueblood's white woman again steps out of the clock's frame. "It was like a dream interval," Invisible Man reflects, but it was both real and dream, categories the novel gradually erodes.

142

The white woman ceases to unnerve him only when the veil of associations and expectations with which he surrounds her begins to part, and his experience in being mistaken for Rinehart is the necessary prelude to that revelation. In that experience Ellison dramatizes most explicitly that our sense of reality is illusion – *though none the less real for that*. Invisible Man has persistently sought to distinguish between reality and illusion, to pierce the surface to find the substantial depth beneath, but he misunderstands the black doctor's advice and begins to intuit this fact only when he dons the dark green glasses that cause him to be confused with Rinehart. For the first time in the novel he is trying not to be seen, but this too is a joke, since he has been invisible all along. This irony is underlined by Invisible Man's unintentional echo of the veteran's declaration, "You're hidden right out in the open – that is, you would be if you only realized it" (152). His green glasses do hide him "right in front of their eyes" (474), but they conceal another mask, not a true self that is invisible without them.

The Rinehart episode is not without its lessons, however. His experience of wearing a mask introduces Invisible Man to the reality of masks and the fluidity of reality: "If dark glasses and a white hat could blot out my identity so quickly, who actually was who?" (482). Moreover, his discovery of the many masks of Rinehart leads him to the suspicion that Rinehart is only a mask, one of Proteus's many changes. "Could he himself be both rind and heart? What is real anyway?" he asks, and then concludes admiringly,

> His world was possibility and he knew it. He was years ahead of me and I was a fool. I must have been crazy and blind. The world in which we lived was without boundaries. A vast seething, hot world of fluidity, and Rine the rascal was at home. Perhaps *only* Rine the rascal was at home in it. It was unbelievable, but perhaps only the unbelievable could be believed. Perhaps the truth was always a lie. (487)

This is the genesis of the oxymoron on which the novel is built, and its immediate consequence is Invisible Man's contempt for the Brotherhood's claim to be following the "laws of reality": "It was all a swindle, an obscene swindle! They had set themselves up to describe the world" (496).

The implications of his rage extend far beyond irritation with how little the Brotherhood knows about the realities of Harlem life, for they undermine the idea of description itself. In this way, the hero's education is the appropriate corollary of the novel's psychological form, which celebrates the hero's escape from the Brotherhood's realist narrative, and shows that description involves both projection and invention in masquerade.

Since one of Ellison's purposes in writing the novel was to take issue with those prevailing descriptions (and their ideological assumptions) that served the white world as images of the real, his own narrative had to avoid the same error of assuming a material, absolute reality to which his language might refer. At the same time, Invisible Man *does* experience the reality of his encounters with the world around him, and that reality – though different for each man or woman – is the psychological relation shared by all, which Ellison sought to express. That this relation may be either imprisoning or liberating is part of the social and political power latent in the ability to tell one's story, and accounts again for Ellison's insistence upon the ambivalence and power of masks.

Despite the apparent insight informing his rage, Invisible Man is not yet entirely free of the naive model of reality that keeps him blind. The fundamental lesson he has drawn from his Rinehart experience is that it is possible to be invisible; although he has been living this fact all along, it is only when he consciously conceals himself that he experiences his invisibility. He determines to make use of this new knowledge by deceiving the Brotherhood. Ellison's control in this latter section of the novel is brilliant, for it appears that Invisible Man has at long last touched down; but when he asks, "now that I had found the thread of reality, how could I hold on?" (500), he shows that he is still securely lodged in the double frame of his own (and his author's) irony.

The actions that follow upon this determination demonstrate that Invisible Man reads the syntax of his phrase "the thread of reality" to emphasize possession and control, which assume a center of authority at the heart of the labyrinth. By following the "thread of reality" he hopes to learn "what actually guided their operations." In his mind, reality is still distinct from his own existence, and finding it is merely a "problem of information" (500). His first efforts to employ this naive idea of action – offering the Brotherhood false membership lists – work almost too well, for they are received and made use of without the blinking of an eye: "Illusion was creating a counter-illusion" (504). But when he seduces Sybil, one of the "big shot's wives," in the hope that she will prove to be an oracle and give him access to the Brotherhood's plan, he is once again rebuffed.

Secure in the knowledge of his invisibility, Invisible Man enters upon his evening with the last avatar of the novel's white goddess, but in this scene Ellison shows the goddess to be a figure existing only in the psychological territory of the novel's deluded characters. Throughout the book, she has been thought of as the sexual power at the center of all control and planning; but Sybil is no oracle, source neither of information nor of revelation. Like Norton in the Golden Day, she is just a human being. When Invisible Man says to her, "Tell me about George. Tell me about that great master mind of social change," she expresses disbelief: "Who, *Georgie?* . . . Georgie's blind'sa mole in a hole'n doesn't know a thing about it" (513). This itself, of course, is a partial revelation; additionally, Sybil's own humanity finally impresses itself on him despite her failure to see him: "What had I done to her, allowed her to do?" Having learned to use his mask of invisibility, he now learns the responsibility of masks. Though invisible, he is not without the power to affect others.

By this point in the novel, readers may have become impatient with the failure of Invisible Man's recurring insights to pay off in strategic dividends, but this final gambit is rendered ineffective because Ellison is trying to bring down bigger game than the Brotherhood, and *his* strategy is the progressive disillusionment of his character. Each disillusionment involves the removal of another mask, revealing the successive surfaces of the world – instead of discovering an origin of power and reality outside himself. Within this larger context, the Brotherhood – most narrowly, a parody of the left in the United States during the thirties – is only a figure for the force that the veteran refers to as "They": "the same *they* we always mean, the white folks, authority, the gods, fate, circumstances – the force that pulls your strings until you refuse to be pulled any more" (152).

The veteran's words should remind readers of the "doll's mask" of the nude dancer, first of the novel's puppets, and they point to the fact that so long as Invisible Man imagines that reality is to be found at the end of Ariadne's thread, he too will be only a doll. The complex significance of the phrase "thread of reality" – anticipated in the dancer's motions and the vet's figure of speech – thus involves the relations of mask, reality, and power; and those relations are most fully dramatized in the scene of Tod Clifton's demise.

Tod Clifton, we may recall, has been the handsome face of the Brotherhood (just as Invisible Man has been its eloquent spokesman). When Invisible Man discovers him peddling Sambo dolls, he is stupefied that Tod should have chosen to "fall outside of *history*," for "only in the Brotherhood could we make ourselves known, could we avoid being empty Sambo dolls. Such an obscene flouncing of everything human!" (424). Invisible Man is unwilling to admit that Tod has recognized his identity as a doll of the Brotherhood, and prefers to make a living by manipulating a mask rather than be the manipulated face of the Brotherhood.

This scene is another example of the novel's precise ambivalence, for Tod's peddling is both an allegory of manipulation and a model of reality as the relationship between the private self and its public mask. Ellison's tripartite model – self, thread, and mask – allows him to maintain a connection between formlessness (of self and world) and order (of the public mask operating within social form). The connecting thread can be manipulated from either end: One may choose the mask by which he makes his way in the world and thus participate in constituting his reality, or one may accept the mask he is given, in which case his strings are being pulled by a power that remains hidden, "out there." Though Invisible Man at first fails to see the connection between Tod and the dancing dolls, he later finds the "fine black thread" that had made them move. This connecting thread, moreover, had been "invisible," and these two characteristics – connectedness and invisibility – are the central qualities of the phrase Invisible Man later misinterprets, "the thread of reality."

The discovery of the black thread enables Invisible Man to make the doll come to life, to maintain an erect, "taut" posture, for this thread is the invisible connective on which life itself depends. The thread of reality joining self and mask is also that invisible present connecting future possibility with past form, so that the idea of the mask in Ellison's thinking is central not only to the self but to the development of social identity as well. In the Introduction to *Shadow and Act,* Ellison wrote that "here the question of reality and personal identity merge" (xx), for both exist as a process of successive masking that brings a temporary but necessary order out of chaos.

The relations of personal and social identity, implicit throughout the novel, are made explicit in the final scene of the story Invisible Man has to tell. Ellison's emphasis upon reality as process leads him to submit his character to a final disillusionment — necessary to complete the dematerialization of Invisible Man's assumptions — which occurs in the castration dream that closes the interior narrative. In addition to providing a kind of curtain call for all of the novel's major figures and dramatizing their sustained manipulation of Invisible Man, this scene emphasizes the transient relationship of the individual body to the process of the social organism. Having castrated him and tossed his parts up onto the Washington Bridge, Brother Jack asks, "How does it feel to be free of one's illusions?" Typically, Ellison's ambivalent language cuts at least two ways, for Jack's question assumes, on the one hand, that Invisible Man is now faced with reality, whereas, on the other, it points to the idea that reality is made of illusion; and it is this illusion-making power to reproduce that Invisible Man — in his dream — has lost. But in his lost seed, Invisible Man sees a waste not only of personal but of social possibilities as well. The Washington Bridge, which leads from black Harlem to white Jersey, becomes for him an image of humanity's effort to overcome the flow and diversity of life: *"the bridge seemed to move off to where I could not see, striding like a robot, an iron man, whose iron legs clanged doomfully as it moved."* Moving off to where he cannot see, the bridge suggests a sterile, white, machinelike future. Invisible Man's response (*"No, no, we must stop him!"*) calls for collective action because he realizes that personal and social development

147

are inseparable, that both the body of the self and the body politic have substance only in what gives them body, which is the power to embody, to generate and create continuity.

The body, then, is a kind of mask, participating in a succession that is reality. This is not a denial of masks but an affirmation of their inevitability and necessity. One of Invisible Man's college teachers – revising Stephen Dedalus – had suggested as much, but at the time he hadn't understood: The problem of the black man is that of "creating the uncreated features of his face. . . . We create the race by creating ourselves" (346). Ellison insists only that such masks be worn with a degree of irony, for "the mind that has conceived a plan of living must never lose sight of the chaos against which that pattern was conceived. That goes for societies as well as for individuals" (567). This requires developing a tolerance for contradiction and ambiguity, and thus for a complicated idea of freedom and action; but without this tolerance human action – liberal, as well as fascist or communist – remains a kind of sleepwalking, "making a mess of the world" (558).

Not only is the mask the inescapable means by which we have being in the world and are enabled to act, but the mask – as it was for Yeats – is also an instrument of imagination and change. As Invisible Man's closing admonition makes clear, this capacity has ramifications for both individual and national identity. Ellison found a familiar passage from Yeats's autobiography useful for explaining this dual importance of masks:

> There is a relation between discipline and the theatrical sense. If we cannot imagine ourselves as different from what we are and assume that second self, we cannot impose a discipline upon ourselves, though we may accept one from others. Active virtue as distinguished from the passive acceptance of a current code is therefore theatrical, consciously dramatic, the wearing of a mask. It is the condition of arduous full life. (*SA*, 53)[18]

Ellison finds Yeats's view especially appropriate for describing the experience of Americans, who, by throwing off their identity as colonials, had necessarily assumed the discipline of a second mask in order to invent for themselves a new identity. This is the particularly American "joke" that always lies between appearance and reality, and this is the joke whose dynamic ironies are the reality of

Invisible Man, peeking out from behind every ambivalent surface of the novel.

Invisible Man is thus a novel whose imaginative project involves an act of leadership, for its hero's education requires that he imagine himself as other than what he is taken to be, and that education – dramatized as the novel – is an invitation to reconstitute the American experiment in equality and diversity. Ellison has said that while he was writing the novel he was "speculating on the nature of Negro leadership in the United States" (*SA,* 176) and its failure to offer an alternative image of the black man. The novel offers the alternative of an articulate consciousness from its opening self-assertion, "I am an invisible man," and expresses Ellison's determination to "explore the full range of American Negro humanity and to affirm those qualities which are of value beyond any question of segregation, economics or previous condition of servitude" (*SA,* 17) – which is to say, beyond those "deterministic" terms that whites and blacks alike have used to interpret black culture and identity.

However, given both the context of his time – in which collective action seemed at best inept and at worst totalitarian – and the vision of existence that underlies his conception of identity, Ellison found it necessary to frame his portrait of leadership in negative terms. Throughout the novel Invisible Man has wanted to be a leader, but the paradoxical dilemma that increasingly paralyzes him is the question of how to be a leader without by that very act falsifying his mission, how to accept a position from the world he is trying to change without also undermining any hope of credible leadership. All of his efforts have brought him into contact with the major institutions of society and their corrupt leaders: school (Norton, Bledsoe), industrial capitalism (Emerson), political parties (Brother Jack), and race organizing (Ras the Exhorter). Thus, Invisible Man is able to lead only when he conceives of his project negatively. Facing Ras the Exhorter and his men, Invisible Man "recognized them at last as those whom I had failed and of whom I was now, just now, a leader, though leading them, running ahead of them, only in the stripping away of my illusionment" (546).

This negative leadership has led several readers to conclude that

149

Invisible Man fails to mend the divisions it dramatizes and so falsifies the hero's closing affirmations.[19] In this view, Invisible Man ends as paralyzed as Trueblood says he had been, left on the verge of a "second self," which Ellison seems unable to invent. Instead, Invisible Man has been reduced to a disembodied voice. All else, we are given to understand, is illusion: "I've come a long way from those days when, full of illusion, I lived a public life and attempted to function under the assumption that the world was solid and all the relationships therein" (563). Though he says that "the old fascination with playing a role" has returned (566), Ellison seems to have cut the ground from beneath him, for how can a disembodied voice be "socially responsible"? The social reality upon which the novel is so evidently predicated has had its apparent depth gutted by the hero's penetrating insight, and the hero – having accepted his invisibility – has only partial, inadequate being, seeming to hanker for activity on a stage of social theatrics in which he no longer believes.

Invisible Man overcomes these reservations only when the novel's existence is granted reality as the embodiment of its invisible hero. If the language of the novel is viewed as a transparent medium through which we "see" Invisible Man, then the character at the end of the novel is in fact without full being. He is only a voice in need of a body in order to exist in historical social time. Prior to such incarnation, Invisible Man doesn't exist except as a kind of absence or negativity, but this negativity is the very source of his existence for us – present only as the language that gives him being in our world. This is the far end of the logic with which Ellison has pursued the idea of the mask, for just as the wearing of a mask is the enabling discipline of self and society, so is the act of narration the means by which the speaker acquires a second self. In *Invisible Man*, telling one's own story is the wearing of a mask, and such telling is the enabling instrument by which such figures as Trueblood and Brother Tarp manage to retain a sense of themselves apart from the controlling images others have of them. Their self-possession is a form of the freedom that the old black woman in Invisible Man's drug-induced dream defined as "nothing but knowing how to say what I got up in my head" (11). When Norton and Invisible Man listen to Trueblood, his voice takes "on a deep, incantatory quality, as though he had told the story many, many times'' (53), and Brother Tarp, telling the story of his escape from prison, exclaims at one point, ''I'm tellin' it better'n I ever thought I could'' (379). These are the true leaders of the book; Invisible Man joins their company through the self-authorship such telling entails.

Certainly, Ellison's novel may be read as a story about the world of a character whom we know as Invisible Man, but the novel fails to substantiate its own vision unless we shift our attention from the reality the story is ''about'' to the reality of the story. Even as a story ''about,'' of course, the novel is a reflection only of a fictional world, but that world, already past, is only a stage in the process the novel enacts. Invisible Man has prepared himself for his next ''role'' by telling us his experience, but this act of self-generation (by which he becomes, as the vet had advised him, his own father) is a succeeding experience that exerts its influence in turn. In this way, the form of the novel is not merely that of a framed tale, but one that continues to outstrip itself in a spiraling motion. Closing with the hero's incipient emergence – like Thoreau leaving Walden – emphasizes the border between chaos and order as the complex territory of human ambiguity and keeps the novel in motion, faithful to its vision of a world no longer solid. Invisible Man continually renews his relation to the world, and from this standpoint his story about himself describes a prior, accumulated reality that he now sheds (''I'm shaking off the old skin,'' he says), exchanging one mask for another, an exchange that evolves, appropriately, from within.[20]

This Emersonian, expressive idea of reality is radically allied in the novel with the example of Frederick Douglass – whose portrait hangs in Brother Tarp's office and whose doctrine of leadership was based upon self-assertion.[21] It is within this tradition that Invisible Man finally places himself, and his self-assertion within the novel coincides with the anterior act of authorship executed by Ellison himself. The novel, thought of as enclosing the narrator, who encloses his own story, is another mask through which Ellison acquires a public identity and exerts his leadership. This autobiographical aspect of the novel-as-mask, everywhere implicit, is subtly confirmed by the number of lights that line Invisible

151

Man's den. The peculiar specificity of the number — 1,369 — accords well enough with the hero's desperate frame of mind, but because these lights are an image of self-awareness, it is not surprising that in them Ellison should have coded his own initials. At the time he completed the novel, Ellison was thirty-seven years old; by squaring that number, we find the number of lights that give Invisible Man his form. Perhaps Ellison's use of the exponential figure is a metaphor for the power of reflection; a thirty-seven-year-old in the act of writing brings to his work the experience of his thirty-seven years, and the fitting result of his effort is not a sum, but a square. "Fiction," Ellison wrote, "became the agency of my efforts to answer the questions: Who am I, what am I, how did I come to be?" (*SA*, xvii); and the answer his hero finally declares is that he is all that he has been: "I saw that they were more than separate experiences. They were me; they defined me. I was my experiences and my experiences were me" (*IM*, 496). His realization is not only memory but creation, and demonstrates the power of the imagination to give narrative to one's life. It is that created life that is real and whose light "confirms [his] reality, gives birth to [his] form" (*IM*, 6), and that is, quite palpably, the novel itself.

This reality is implicit in the novel's first words, "I am an invisible man," which announce the phenomenological status of all printed voices; but here, with their defiant self-assertion (as words), they insist upon a rejection of any reference to a bodily form other than their own. Any socially responsible role the voice might play depends upon that rejection and its effective autonomy, for this is the source of its integrity and its capacity to lead. The imagination of the novel's voice, then, is not only the genesis of its self-identity (being, as it were, all imagination) but is also a means of renewing America's dream of equality and diversity. "I learned very early," Ellison said in an interview, "that in the realm of the imagination all people and their ambitions and interests could meet" (*SA*, 12). Without this common ground, the culture is in perpetual danger of hardening about an idea it mistakes for reality, and thus exerting a repressive conformity upon all invisible men. This is the universal truth expressed by the novel's autonomy.

Only in that sense is the voice that speaks to us a mimetic device, calling attention to an invisible reality recognizable to all.

To the disembodied voice, sound is the natural medium by which he shares this communal territory. Because the visual sense relies upon surfaces whose associations blind the "inner eyes," the hero appeals to the blues tradition and (more immediately) to sound itself as the means of penetrating those surfaces to reach his blind audience. His metaphor of sound – he calls his silent printed voice the "music of invisibility" – reminds us that *Invisible Man* is one of the last novels written before the era of television, when radio was still the means by which people invisible to each other could share a common world. In the jazz rhyming of the last paragraphs (whose punning improvises upon the ambiguities of "playing" as both social role and private performance), Ellison and his hero coincide in the role of disc jockey, inviting us to tune in to a lower frequency on a neglected part of the band, to find there, in the very midst of what Trilling would later call the "culture's hum and buzz of implication," a different space and time. Here the hero-as-novel executes a stunning reversal, having become host to the society that had held him hostage. By speaking to an invisible consensus, the voice proclaims another community; his suggestion that he speaks for us is a contemporary (and thus hesitant) echo of Emerson's faith in the poet, who, by looking deeply within himself, finds what is true for all men.

NOTES

1. See Robert O'Meally, *The Craft of Ralph Ellison* (Cambridge, Mass: Harvard University Press, 1980), p. 30.
2. Ralph Ellison, *Shadow and Act* (New York: Vintage Books, 1972), p. 102. This volume will be cited hereafter as *SA*.
3. "Eccentrics' Pilgrimage," *Hudson Review*, 6 (Spring 1953):145. Something of the fifties revulsion toward the naive politics of the thirties is still evident in Richard Chase's approval of the novel's portrayal of the "mystery, suffering, transcendent reality, and the ultimate contradictions of life." "A Novel Is a Novel," *Kenyon Review*, 14, (Autumn 1952):678–84. Stephen Spender was more explicit: "His great

achievement is that he is not content to be a 'social realist' learning the lesson of oppression and building up a solid case against social evil." "New Novels," *The Listener,* 49 (January 1953):115.

4. Irving Howe's review was generally favorable, but he took issue with the hero's assertion of freedom: "Though the unqualified assertion of individuality is at the moment a favorite notion of literary people, it is also a vapid one." "A Negro in America," *The Nation,* 174 (May 1952):454. For a catalogue of the case against Ellison, see Ernest Kaiser's "A Critical Look at Ellison's Fiction and at Social and Literary Criticism By and About the Author," *Black World* 20, no. 2 (December 1970):53–9, 81–97.

5. Philip Rahv, *Image and Idea* (Norfolk, Conn.: New Directions, 1949), p. 138.

6. Lionel Trilling, *The Liberal Imagination* (New York: Viking Press, 1950), p. 212.

7. *The Living Novel,* ed. Granville Hicks (New York: Macmillan, 1957), p. 75.

8. See Henry Adams, *The Education of Henry Adams* (New York: Modern Library, 1931), p. 288. The quotation from George Santayana comes from "The Genteel Tradition in American Philosophy," in *Winds of Doctrine* (New York: Charles Scribner's Sons, 1926), p. 207.

9. This bizarrely lighted den is clearly an inverted allegory of the Christian imagery that associates light with God's creation of form and order. Invisible Man's "visibility" is self-created. Compare Augustine:

> Assuredly, this earth was invisible and without order, and there was I know not what profound abyss, upon which there was no light, because there was no form in it. Whence you commanded it to be written that "darkness was upon the deep." What else was this but absence of light? If there were light, what else would it be except up above, standing visible and shedding its rays? (*The Confessions of St. Augustine,* Book 12, chap. 3)

Ellison's use of these symbols not only places the light beneath, rather than "above"; it places the light within, though it is important to note that the power for Invisible Man's light comes from the outside. See the following discussion. Compare Stepto, on "Making Light of the Light," *From Behind the Veil: A Study of Afro-American Narrative* (Urbana: University of Illinois Press, 1979), pp. 175–94.

10. See O'Meally, *The Craft,* p. 78: "As if in defiance of the single-minded critic, Ellison drew symbols and rhetorical schemes from any and

every source he felt would enrich the texture and meaning of his first novel's prose.''

11. See Washington, ''The Atlanta Exposition Address,'' in *Up From Slavery* (New York: Bantam Books, 1959), p. 156; and DuBois, in his chapter about the failure of black leadership, ''Of Mr. Booker T. Washington and Others,'' in *The Souls of Black Folk* (Greenwich, Conn.: Fawcett Publications, 1961), pp. 42–54. No reader of *Invisible Man* can study these pages without realizing the great influence they had on Ellison's novel.

12. See O'Meally, ''The Lure of the Left,'' *The Craft*, pp. 37–55, and Kaiser, ''A Critical Look.''

13. Richard Wright, *Native Son* (New York: Harper & Row, 1966), pp. xxi, xx, xxix, xxxiii.

14. One of the persistent figures of speech in *The Souls of Black Folk* is the ''veil'' that shuts out the Negro from the world: ''the Negro is a sort of seventh son, born with a veil, and gifted with second-sight in the American world — a world which yields him no true self-consciousness, but only lets him see himself through the revelation of the other world'' (p. 16). An apter description of Invisible Man's condition is hard to imagine, and indeed, DuBois's imprint is everywhere in Ellison's book. Consider the ''Sorrow Songs'' that head each of DuBois's chapters and are a kind of ''music of invisibility,'' his emphasis upon ''self-assertion'' (p. 47), and his belief that the future of ''the darker races'' rests ''so largely upon this American experiment'' (p. 51). Perhaps Ellison set himself the task of answering the white man's question that DuBois poses at the beginning of his essay: ''To the real question, How does it feel to be a problem? I seldom answer a word'' (p. 15). Though little has been written on the relationship between DuBois and Ellison, Stepto's *From Behind the Veil* offers an excellent discussion of Ellison's alteration of DuBois's characteristic figures and strategies.

15. In another novel about an ambitious young man from the country, Julien Sorel felt ''he was at last going to appear on the stage of great events.'' *The Red and the Black* (New York: Random House, 1953), p. 272.

16. Chase, ''A Novel is a Novel,'' p. 681.

17. Hicks, *The Living Novel*, p. 63.

18. *The Autobiography of William Butler Yeats* (New York: Macmillan, 1953), p. 285.

19. See, for example, Irving Howe's well-known essay, ''Black Boys and

Native Sons," in *A World More Attractive* (New York: Horizon Press, 1963); Ernest Kaiser's "A Critical Look at Ellison's Fiction and at Social and Literary Criticism by and about the Author," *Black World* 20, no. 2 (December 1970):53–9, 81–97; and Eleanor Wilner, "The Invisible Black Thread: Identity and Nonentity in *Invisible Man*," *CLA Journal*, 13, (March 1970):242–57, for whom the hero "remains identified with a role, the role of nonentity" and thus the novel fails "to digest the material of its own vision" (256, 243).

20. The echoes of *Walden* are numerous and specific: Invisible Man's "moulting season" has been a "crisis" in his life, which has helped him discard an "exogenous" existence "by an internal industry and expansion." Like Thoreau, Invisible Man leaves his "hibernation" either in the "Spring" or the "hope of Spring." As in Thoreau's "excrementitious" Spring, Invisible Man notes "there's a stench in the air" (567).

21. See DuBois, "Washington," p. 47. See also Robert Stepto on Ellison's use of "portrait galleries" in "Literacy and Hibernation: Ralph Ellison's *Invisible Man*," *The Carleton Miscellany*, 18 (Winter 1980):112–41.

6

The Conscious Hero and the Rites of Man: Ellison's War

JOHN S. WRIGHT

THE psychogenesis of *Invisible Man*, Ralph Ellison has reiterated periodically, lies in a World War II furlough's tonic state of "hyperreceptivity": Sent home from the Merchant Marines in the winter of 1944 to recuperate from wartime stress, Ellison had "floundered" into a powerful intuition. With the aesthetic conviction that "war could, with art, be transformed into something more meaningful than its surface violence" (*IM* p. xiv), he had begun work on a recalcitrant war novel. That work was subverted, he says, by a punning inner voice that brooded over the perennial conundrum of black soldiers fighting for the right to fight for freedom in a war designed to return them home unfree. The voice announced irrepressibly, "I am an invisible man." Its words rebutted sharply the sociological truism that most Afro-American troubles sprang from the group's "high visibility," and spurred Ellison to abandon his planned war novel for a highly experimental, panoramic, and picaresque fictional "memoir." The new work concerned itself more broadly "with the nature of leadership, and thus with the nature of the hero . . . [and] with the question of just why our Negro leadership was never able to enforce its will. Just what was there about American society that kept Negroes from throwing up effective leaders?"[1] Absorbed at the same moment with Lord Raglan's *The Hero: A Study in Tradition, Myth, and Drama* (1936), Ellison turned his explorations into modern myth, mores, and caste codes to the specific subject of American "race rituals." His probings subsequently yielded, as a narrative embryo, the grotesque high school graduation rites undergone by a young, would-be leader of his people in the tale "Battle Royal," which Ellison

157

published in 1947, five years before the novel for which it would serve as the opening chapter.

With riffs on Lord Raglan's myth of heroic biography guiding the ritual understructure, and with "Battle Royal" as a reverberating point of entry, Ellison devised a carefully articulated skeleton for the body of the narrative he then encircled with Prologue and Epilogue:

> I began with a chart of the three-part division. It was a conceptual frame with most of the ideas and some incidents indicated. The three parts represent the narrator's movement from, using Kenneth Burke's terms, purpose to passion to perception. These three major sections are built up of smaller units of three which mark the course of the action. . . . The maximum insight on the hero's part isn't reached until the final section. After all, it's a novel about innocence and human error, a struggle through illusion to reality. Each section begins with a sheet of paper; each piece of paper is exchanged for another and contains a definition of his identity, or the social role he is to play as defined for him by others. But all say essentially the same thing, "Keep this nigger boy running." Before he could have some voice in his own destiny he had to discard these old identities and illusions: his enlightenment couldn't come until then.[2]

The "blues-toned laughter-at-wounds" Ellison created to narrate the tale serves as the controlling consciousness of the underground memoir. But his "identity" is only nominally its subject: The functional subject is the proper conduct of his battle royal for freedom and full consciousness in a modern picaresque world. This world of flux and contradiction is one where identity itself is strategy more than entity and where selfhood is a synonym for improvisation. As if in illustration of Clausewitz's psychology of guerrilla war (the first American translations of Clausewitz's *On War* appeared during World War II and selectively infiltrated the warborn novels of the era), the narrator's wounding movement toward enlightenment reveals progressively the psychic need for the materially weak to be morally strong in the face of an adversary and to subordinate potentially suicidal military conflict to social, political, and economic engagements. Ultimately, the invisible man is locked in a war of wills, and his attempt to master society's meanings and patterns, to acquire a conscious philosophy and a pragmatic code of living in it – and to lead – become an inadvertent Clausewitzian study in the conduct of war by other means. His is a struggle to keep the will to struggle from being destroyed by an ambiguous enemy's insidious psychological warfare.

In this connection, the legacy of the War between the States is one of the great understated themes of *Invisible Man*. The dramatic historical reversals, from Civil War battlefields to Reconstruction politics to Reconstruction's subversion in turn by armed terrorism and political compromise, are reconstituted here in the riddling "orders" the hero's dying grandfather bequeathes him. And they are evoked in the old man's fierce divulgence to all of his heirs that "our life is a war and I have been a traitor all my born days, a spy in the enemy's country ever since I give up my gun back in the Reconstruction" (16).

These words announce the novel's partisan premise that, with giving up the gun, politics necessarily becomes the substitute for war – and potentially its antidote. And that premise shapes how Ellison adapts the conventions of the picaresque and of heroic myth. The world of *Invisible Man* re-creates the familiar warring society of picaresque – only nominally civilized, a scene where life, death, incest, fornication, treachery, insanity, prostitution, labor strife, scatology, mutilation, political violence, and riot are all inescapably intermingled. And in a society so construed, the true rogue-picaro – the con man Rinehart – is the ultimate warrior and predator. It is he who rules as subversive antitype to Lord Raglan's hero of tradition, originally a royal warrior on an epic quest and an unquestioned embodiment of his future kingdom's deepest religious and political values. Historically, the unpredatory picaresque alternative to the destructive rogue from the social underground has been a rational, upwardly mobile potential bourgeois, one whose roguery is less criminality than pragmatism: more a maneuvering around obstacles to his full assimilation into society than an attempt to destroy society itself.

In neither incarnation was the modern picaro necessarily a conscious rebel; and even when most subversive, he or she was never politically oriented. Moreover, the picaresque hero had little sense of community or family and was too engrossed in the arduous struggle to survive and win the social war to seek any satisfactions in heterosexual love beyond the merely biological or honorific. Caught up in the pressures of the present, he lacked any abstract sense of the macrocosmic workings of society and any historical consciousness.[3] In American fiction, Mark Twain's moralized use of picaresque conventions in *Huckleberry Finn* incorporated the picaro as an obstreperous contra-bourgeois white-trash scamp who remains "preideological" as well as ultimately unamenable to life within society. In *Invisible Man*, by contrast, Ellison's commitment is to a formally educated black protagonist, politically impassioned and struggling toward philosophical awareness. He is a rising bourgeois hero, closer to Quixote, Candide, Gulliver, or Melville's Ishmael than to a rogue – though he is ultimately impelled to roguery by circumstance. For this hero, even temporary life outside society finally becomes untenable; indeed, for him the animating goal is that of public leadership – the preeminently bourgeois aspiration that appears most typically in picaresque narrative as an object of ridicule.

What indeed is programmatically ridiculous about the situation of Ellison's invisible man derives from his being, functionally, the bourgeois hero of a *Bildungsroman* displaced, incongruously, into the realm of the picaresque. His apprenticeship to life and leadership, in the lenient logic of *Bildungsroman*, would have allowed him numerous mistakes of judgment and repeated chances to right himself without experiencing undue suffering. Instead, his "education" is hyperbolized, by the brutal logic of picaresque, into a chronicle of comic catastrophe; and he is caught in a labyrinth where his errors unerringly cause him pain and where only a true picaro, who is *born* knowing and needs no education, would not err. The heroic expectation of overcoming and the comic hope of not being overcome collide at nearly every point of crisis in Ellison's black and blue tragicomedy, crisis determined here neither by episodic happenstance nor naturalistic law but by the alternate and no less rigid determinism of the ritual process. The narrative patterns of heroic myth and of the picaresque converge in this context. For the picaresque, even without the schematic mythology Ellison employs, characteristically retains elements of ritual, especially rites of passage, which test, often mock-heroically, its protagonist's "mother wit" and wisdom.[4]

Ellison's protagonist, more pointedly than other laughers-at-wounds with whom he is compared all along his road of trials, is, from his rude southern beginnings to his rising fame and fall up North, a thoroughgoing mock-heroic counterpart to Lord Raglan's hero of tradition. With a slave's genealogy of shame to mark and mock him, and with no dynastic family traditions save his ex-slave grandfather's secret roles as traitor and spy and agent provocateur, he enters the world "no freak of nature or of history" but born of parents who are, if not unknown, then unnamed and otherwise unnecessary to his ritual progress. His preinvisible childhood days are a blank spent miming his grandfather's steely meekness until vague promptings to leadership propel him, as initiate, into the nightmarish battle royal of life. With his grandfather's riddling counsel still to be deciphered along the way, and the word magic of his native oratorical powers to sustain him, he moves away from the seemingly stable and naturalistic world of the rural South and Negro mis-education (really a semifeudal "flower studded wasteland" seething with disorder). Fortuitously deceived, he embarks on a journey *up North* geographically but *down* existentially into a netherworld of human and mechanical monsters and mis-leaders who preside over surreal forms of establishment and anti-establishment chaos. In his search for a place in the world, he finds himself unceasingly embattled, alone, and *dis*placed. Outside the maze of *mis*namings that his treacherous allies lay before him, he remains nameless. His own self-chosen moniker – a mock *title*, not simply a name – links him to a mock kingdom by way of a salient greeting–response ritual common in 1930s and 1940s black communities: "How are you?" The response: "Like Jack-the-Bear: just ain't nowhere" (*SA,* 297).

He is, however, succored at crucial junctures by symbolic foster parents and by the survival wisdom of the maternal folk community he at first foolishly repudiates but ultimately reaffirms. He wins all of his victories through such self-affirming eloquence as he commands, and all of his reverses spring from self-negating acquiescence. He rises to a brief reign as orator-king over an up-town realm of restive Harlem subjects. In turn, he is deposed suddenly by his treacherous "Brothers," exiled downtown to what the Brotherhood considers to be the ideological backwaters of the

"Woman Question," and finally he vanishes, first, metaphysically, into the urban wonderland behind a pair of magical sunglasses and then literally, when driven underground by his rebellious subjects and into sepulchral hibernation. Ultimately, he resurrects himself from the ashes of his political failures and personal dissimulations by inscribing a "code of laws" in the form of his codified life – the memoir of a ranter turned writer.

If Ellison has given his narrator all of these ritual trappings of the mock-mythical hero, the context enforces riffing variations on Raglan's biographical pattern. The hero's potentially Oedipal antagonism toward the father-king and his desire for the surrogate mother-queen are inverted sexually, for the king to be deposed and his potential deposer are crossed in Jack-the-Bear's world by racial as well as incest taboo. The same antagonism is deflected politically, because Ellison's rising hero *misleads himself* repeatedly not to rule but to be ruled. A rabble-rouser, not a warrior, he makes speeches instead of making war; and he fails his many trials comically more than tragically because all of his reverses are self-generated "boomerangs" – bruising but inconsequential pratfalls. A creature of the age of mass ideology and modern technology, he models a comedy at the brink of tragedy that is less akin to Odysseus's heroic saga of comic wiliness and adaptability, or to Aristotle's comic "species of the ugly which is not painful," than to the image Ellison found in Henri Bergson's *Laughter* of human behavior become mechanized, rigid, life-denying, robotic, and hence comically maladjusted.

If Jack-the-Bear is not the martial hero fated to found kingdoms, destroy his enemies, kill his father, or dispel plagues, neither is he the rutting picaresque hero of play and waggish sensuality, prone to the pleasures of the senses and the lure of bawd and belle alike. *Politics* is his passion, ritualized and romanticized. And he disciplines himself against dissipation, averring in youth his college roommate's more natural passion when "the grass is green" to seek out "broad-butt gals with ball-bearing hips" (*IM*, 104); and weakening in later years only before the pandering allurements of enemy sibyls or to the "political" necessity for fornicational reconnaissance. Through it all, the narrator dimly suspects conspiracy, betrayal, and persecution; but he nearly always disregards all warnings. His unfaced fears are confirmed at the novel's end and reach a crescendo in the castration dream that punctuates his ritual progress.

Ellison's awareness of the suppressed psychic and symbolic "power of blackness"[5] attuned him more than Raglan had been to the dark side of heroic myth, to its demonic and demiurgic possibilities. Accordingly, he found a major role in his conception for what in Raglan's ritual drama had been a minor character: the *Spielman*, a figure half-trickster, half-devil, who, like the Norse god Loki, is the sacred plotter and wily father of artifice who sets the conflict in motion and drags the demons and giants toward their ultimate defeat. And in Mephistophelian fashion, though he plays no part in the drama, the *Spielman* is the motive power behind key characters, inspiring them to tabooed acts and leading them to ruin. As ritual prompter and stage manager appearing in different guises throughout, Ellison's *Spielman* – speaking in the voices of the Prologue's "singer of spirituals," or the Golden Day's mad veteran, or the cartman "Peter Wheatstraw-the-devil's-son-in-law," or Tod Clifton after his plunge outside history, or the omnipresent mocker-mentor figure of the narrator's grandfather – persistently utters the magic words that goad the hero to act.

The invisible man's acts of attempted leadership mark the stages of his ritual progress "from purpose to passion to perception"; they also chronicle his relationships with a procession of post-Reconstruction black leadership archetypes. The narrator's on-going meditations on the methods and mysteries of leadership, the complex patterns of animal and mechanical and aesthetic imagery, and the periodic eruptions of unofficial leadership that counterpoint the parade of official power brokers – all expand his narrative's range of political commentary. *Invisible Man* probes the character of leadership strategies as well as the relationships between the leaders and the led; identifies the spectrum of tactical constraints within which political maneuvers must be devised; and makes utopian as well as pragmatic leadership the object of satiric dissection. A trio of heroic images from the black past – Frederick Douglass, Booker T. Washington, and Marcus Garvey – provide a genealogy of authentic political leaders; and a pantheon of nonpolitical heroes – Louis Armstrong, Paul Robeson, Joe

Louis, John Henry – suggest, if only as names or cameo images, certain attitudes, techniques, and attributes proper to the movers and shakers of humanity.

Quite naturally, the nameless narrator's problem of identity, which is bound up at one level with his progress in reintegrating into his life the traditions of his repressed folk past, on another level must be resolved concretely in the personal drama of his leadership ambitions. One lesson implicit in his boomeranging movement across the social landscape is that the identity he seeks, like the leadership to which he aspires, is not a fixed entity but a pattern of transactions with other people. At its most lifegiving, leadership entails a creatively improvised assertion of the leader's whole self within and against the group will; and at its most eviscerating, it merely camouflages the self's public retreat into sanctioned dissimulation.

As he turns his talent for public oratory into his tool for leading, his attempts to harness the power of words record his slow progress in consciously unifying the elements of his developing will, wisdom, and technique. The bizarre world he inhabits and the role he blunderingly seeks keep these facets of the whole man and the true leader fragmented and at odds. At the town smoker after the humiliating rites of the battle royal, the invisible man "automatically" mouths Booker T. Washington's Atlanta Compromise Address for the unhearing throng of his abusers. His parrotry is a parody of leadership as are his self-avowed "powers of endurance" and naive "belief in the rightness of things." He is, as the Golden Day's mad vet later incisively proclaims, a "walking zombie" who has learned "to repress not only his emotions but his humanity" (92). As willing heir to that "great false wisdom taught slaves and pragmatists alike, that white is right," he is ready to do the bidding of such false gods as the white millionaire philanthropist, Mr. Norton, and his self-anointed appeaser, the black college president, A. Hebert Bledsoe. And it is Bledsoe's mode of leadership as well-heeled sycophancy that claims the leader-neophyte's attention in his college years:

> He was the example of everything I hoped to be: Influential with wealthy men all over the country; consulted in matters concerning the race; a leader of his people; the possessor of not one but *two*

Cadillacs, a good salary and a soft, good-looking and creamy-complexioned wife. (99)

The mastery of oratorical magic that the narrator associates with such leadership is demonstrated most tangibly for him on Founder's Day in the orotund homiletics of the Reverend Homer Barbee. Barbee's sermon is a praise song to the ex-slave-cum-demigod who rose from oppression and obscurity to found a citadel of learning in a hostile wilderness. Barbee has mastered the myth of heroic biography (Ellison vivified Raglan's ritual pattern here in unerring detail) and its officious power in the college's annual "black rites of Horatio Alger." Ellison allows Barbee's oratorical prowess to wax unmocked until the speaker stumbles from the rostrum, revealing his blindness. The author thereby allows the reader to feel with the narrator the full powers of Barbee's eloquence, powers that, though yoked here to a finally delusive vision of the race's history as "a saga of mounting triumphs," nonetheless hold the promise of leadership for whoever might possess them.

Cast out by Bledsoe from that saga's sacred ground, which the invisible man identifies (echoing Candide) as "the best of all possible worlds," he treks north with his confidence and optimism reviving. Not yet aware of how thoroughly he has been betrayed and "kept running," he preserves undimmed his enthusiasm for oratory and the art of leadership. Being a leader is still, he thinks, a matter of "playing a leading role," of learning "the platform tricks of the leading speakers," of affecting an image of sophistication and hygienic respectability, of stage-managing contacts with "big men," and of mastering such Bledsoe-like "secrets of leadership" as cultivating an aura of mysterious profundity to keep oneself omnipresent in the minds of one's inferiors. Nor, he thinks, could a prospective leader give much thought to love, for "in order to travel far, you had to be detached."

But he is driven to a higher level of consciousness by a cumulation of experiences. The first is his workingman's fiasco at Liberty Paints with Lucius Brockaway and at the factory hospital. The next is his deep alienation from the black fantasy world of upwardly mobile posturing and narcotic self-aggrandizement that he encounters among the roomers at the Men's House. Last is his resentment toward Bledsoe, which erupts after the narrator sloughs off repressive bourgeois prohibitions against yam eating and in so doing releases the submerged well of feeling that spurs his virtuoso streetcorner exhortation against the eviction of an elderly black couple. The speech marks his transition from a phase of egocentric leadership "for" society to a phase of self-effacing leadership "against" the social order. And his extemporaneous rhetorical pyrotechnics signal his regenerated political will to freedom and his new mastery of oratorical "technique." At last he unites his own unconstrained psychic experience with the complex symbols of his people's emotional history – which he has now perceptively deciphered in the tangled heap of mementos piled before the dispossessed couple. Consequently, he is able to articulate a transforming vision and move a mass of men and women to action that, for a moment at least, breaks the chain of injustice.

On the basis of this effective fusion of controlled anger, abstract principle, and vernacular style, he is ushered immediately into the politics of the Brotherhood (whose glorification of arch-capitalist Booker T. Washington and whose leader's symbolic Fourth of July birthdate warn against any such easy identification with the Communist Party as readers in search of political scapegoats might wish). Renamed, relocated, reclothed, and initiated into the doctrinal mysteries of "scientific" political theory, the narrator now adopts a new professional leadership role. Ellison dramatizes its successes and tensions in the narrator's subsequent rabble-rousing Brotherhood speeches; in such promotional innovations as his People's Hot Foot Squad and the symbolic posters of a future "Rainbow" coalition of America's races; and ultimately in his funeral oration for his martyred Brotherhood comrade, Tod Clifton. Jack-the-Bear's changing conceptions of leadership mirror his shift of allegiance from the example of the Founder (which he secretly adopts in opposition to the Brotherhood's desire to make him another Washington) to that of Frederick Douglass, whose portrait becomes his personal totem. As he becomes ambitious to rise in the Brotherhood hierarchy – he thinks it the one organization in the country in which he faces "no limits" – such changes in role model signal his growing clashes with the group's depersonalizing rigidity and thinly veiled racism.

The Brotherhood veteran Tod Clifton, symbolically "black-marble"-skinned to the narrator's "ginger" color, and a man of action more than words – handsome, sensual, and with the air of "a hipster, a zoot suiter, a sharpie" – is the "possible rival" who becomes the narrator's true brother and leaderly alter ego. Clifton's tragic plunge outside what the Brotherhood calls "history" sets in motion a chain of events that leads the narrator into self-proclaimed guerrilla war against the Brotherhood and leads the Harlem community into the apocalyptic riots that are triggered, like Clifton's death, by a murderous political logic that betrays the weak and then singles them out to be sacrificed in the name of leadership's "higher law." Swept along in these riots that terminate his tale, cornered and about to be killed by Ras the Destroyer's followers, the narrator finds his apprenticeship in leading finally at an end. And now finally wordless, he faces an angry group of the Harlemites he had hoped to lead as instead

> no hero, but short and dark with only a certain eloquence and a bottomless capacity for being a fool to mark me from the rest; [I] saw them, recognized them at last as those whom I had failed and of whom I was now, just now, a leader, though leading them, running ahead of them, only in the stripping away of my illusionment. (546)

The narrative logic behind his final political failure, however, is not, as so many of Ellison's commentators have somehow concluded, a cumulative determinism that despairingly dooms all of this world's political possibilities to defeat. The logic is rather that of a rigorous Ellisonian phenomenology of consciousness and strategic style, which posits unequivocally a genuine autonomy in the ways individuals and groups *conceive* their experience and *choose* (or fail to choose) ideas, techniques, and attitudes that defy whatever or whoever limits their possibilities.

The limits imposed on black leaders and political action are hyperbolic realities in the world of *Invisible Man*, experienced directly as the powers of persons and contexts to dominate consciousness first of all. In the narrative's southern context, power polarizes between the local black-baiters who orchestrate the battle royal and the northern millionaire impresarios who bankroll black mis-education in the name of manifest destiny. The logic of such limitation drives the conventional black leadership class –

the ex-soldiers, lawyers, politicians, preachers, doctors, teachers, and artists that the narrator encounters at the Golden Day – either into straitjackets and the insane asylum or into the self-humiliating, Janus-faced machinations of a Bledsoe. In the North, the same class, nominally freer and with access to wider strategic alternatives, falls prey to urban alienation and anonymity. They become dissociated from their communities and are forced, by organizational default, to fall in line "like prisoners" to the dictates of outside political directorates like the Brotherhood.

Nor are the prospects for combatting these nightmare conditions any less dreary in a broad national context that seems to offer the narrator

> no possibility of organizing a splinter movement, for what would be the next step? Where would we go? There were no allies with whom we could join as equals; nor were there time or theorists available to work out an over-all program of our own. . . . We had no money, no intelligence apparatus, either in government, business or labor unions; and no communications with our own people except through unsympathetic newspapers, a few Pullman porters who brought provincial news from distant cities, and a group of domestics who reported the fairly uninteresting private lives of their employers. (499–500)

Moreover, the masses, for obscure reasons, but with consequences not obscure at all, seem to *tolerate* the versions of Bledsoe, Ras, Jack, and Rinehart who cynically or romantically exploit them. In dramatizing this perverse mental landscape, Ellison's narrative yields the psychic and material forces of political disintegration a commanding sway – and yields the narrator full consciousness and the ability to articulate it only in retrospect.

Implicit in Jack-the-Bear's growth of perception, however, is a restabilizing calculus that measures each of the leaders or misleaders in the narrative in terms of a complex phenomenological equation that, like a gestalt, treats leadership as an organized whole whose parts belong together and that cannot function otherwise. As a reaction to the specific realities the novel proposes, in other words, true leadership in *Invisible Man* is finally not a matter of political will or technical mastery or ethical values or inspiration or ideology or analytical accuracy or shared sensibilities, but the whole and creative integration of all of these elements into an effective organic response. No stranger to psychological theory, Ellison put Freudian and Jungian concepts and the role psychology of Harry Stack Sullivan to eclectic rhetorical use in his fiction. And for Ellison, the theory of gestalt — unlike the others a psychology of *perception,* and thus directly relevant to his concept of invisibility and his Burkeian view of the ritual process — cogently suggested symbolic techniques for showing his characters in harmonious or unharmonious relationship to their immediate private and political situations. Jack-the-Bear's accounts of his jangling experiences and his political speechmaking accordingly dramatize richly detailed holistic gestalts of physiological, perceptual, syntactic, emotional, and ideological interaction that measure the unity he is able to achieve, as a leader, in the course of persistently *dis*unified events.

The specific import of such a calculus is that it conceives the problem of leadership and the problem of identity as related aspects of the human organism's struggle for creative unification. The parade of mis-leaders we encounter in *Invisible Man* is not one of fixed types representing unambiguously defective philosophies and completely discardable strategies. They are, rather, types of ambiguity, Empsonian in the ways they personify how warring contraries might either be bound up schizophrenically in a single psyche or fused in "antagonistic cooperation" to clarify a complexly unified sensibility. They represent, also, older vernacular or allegorical types of ambiguity that suggest human dispositions strangely distorted, unbalanced, fragmented by some fixed obsession or constitutional disproportion of humors. In Bledsoe, Barbee, Norton, Emerson, Jr., Brockaway, Ras, and Jack, vision and impaired vision coexist, as do reality and unreality, plausible pragmatism and the perversely irrational. Accordingly Bledsoe's highhanded tricksterism evokes the rich history of folk-fable wisdom to lend it credence. Barbee's grandiloquent eulogy of redemptive progress roots itself in faiths indispensable to group and individual effort. And the strategy with which Lucius Brockaway has made John Henry's martyrdom obsolete and himself indispensable to the Machine is a pragmatic though precarious and inevitably paranoid adjustment to life as a black workingman on the horns of the white man's capitalist-unionist dilemma. Similarly, Ras's fervid

Pan Africanism yields accurate assessments of white men's treachery, even though it is blended with a violently quixotic atavism whose results are "not funny, or not only funny, but dangerous as well, wrong but justified, crazy and yet coldly sane" (552). Even Brother Jack's mechanistic theory of life as all pattern and discipline and science, though fascistically brutal, conveys truths without which organized political action is inconceivable.

Yet measured against Ellison's paradigmatic leadership gestalt, all of these mis-leaders and their dispositions are absurdly neurotic and politically inadequate representatives of a fractured humanity. Worshippers of control and manipulation, all are rigid, robotized, automatic types, unadaptive and painfully comic in the Bergsonian sense; partisans of some merely provisional tactic or ideology unsuited to endure change or to ensure dignity, incapable of conceiving the world in all of its fluid reality, much less of transforming it creatively.

In the South, Trueblood's dream-driven act of incest provides a point of gestaltic convergence triangulated by the competing imperatives of the three mis-leaders who control the sharecropper's peasant existence: first, the landowning southern whites who, led by the "boss man" and the sheriff, intercede for Trueblood and make his "unnatural act" of incest a cause for celebration; second, the moneyed northerners who, in the person of Mr. Norton, atone for betraying Trueblood's ancestral Reconstruction dream of forty acres and a mule by converting the reprobate farmer's sexual misfortune into a hundred-dollar scapegoat ritual; and third, the black college people on the hill who, as the narrator confesses, "hated the blackbelt people, the 'peasants,'" for returning the college's efforts to uplift them by doing, "like Trueblood, . . . everything, it seemed, to pull us down" (47).

Trueblood's relationships with each side of this triumvirate reveal the political truths behind his metaphorical self-identification with the powerless but still perceiving jaybird he describes, who is paralyzed by yellow jacket stings "but still alive in his eyes and . . . watchin' 'em sting his body to death" (62). The southern whites regularly confirm their *power* to rule with such rites as the battle royal and with such bestowals of feudal largesse as sending the scholarship-winning narrator to his mis-education. More cru-

170

cially, they confirm their delusory *right* to rule with the kind of symbolic magic Trueblood has "accidentally" ceded them by dreaming into being the perversity of his life. And as Trueblood's perverse mishap confirms the power of the southerners to re-enslave him, it confirms the impotence, conversely, of northern liberalism to free him. For the first fruit Mr. Norton will see of his investments in the Founder's effort to transform "barren clay to fertile soil" is Trueblood's harvest of sexual sin. That harvest, at the sharecropper's cabin initially and later at the Golden Day, is shown to be, for Norton and his Emersonian ministry no less than for Trueblood and his star-crossed family, a "black 'bomination . . . birthed to bawl [his] wicked sin befo' the eyes of God" (66).

Concomitantly, the black college "power house" on the hill, which closes the third side of the triangle around Trueblood's emblematic life, sustains *its* power with rites of leadership that, again, expropriate and alienate Trueblood's peasant community rather than serve and empower it. Ellison's narrative carefully distinguishes the historical personage of Booker T. Washington from that of the fictional Founder and the Founder's protégé, Bledsoe. But all three are representatives of the same overarching philosophy of racial uplift that historically dominated southern black education during the age of Booker T. Washington. And Jim Trueblood, in the rhetoric Washington so assiduously cultivated, is the novel's primary embodiment of that "man farthest down" for whom the buckets of racial uplift ostensibly are to be lowered. Yet as Trueblood relates, he once had gone to the Founder's college for book learning and for help with his crops. But instead of lead-ership, he had received contempt and ridicule, subsequently losing his land and his independence in the course of the college's rise to nominal power – and so ironically being lowered into disgrace instead of being lifted to liberty.

The deified Founder in whose name the sharecropper has quite literally been sacrificed – Trueblood's "primitive spirituals" are appropriated to sanctify the "black rites of Horatio Alger" and his public shame extirpated from the college's official consciousness – is no mere apostle of wealth or prestige. He is an energetic cult's supreme oracle and avatar, wielding "the power of a king, or in a sense, a god," one who presumably rules benevolently, through

faith, not fear. His "living agent," Bledsoe, however, has converted the Founder's utopian vision into a cynical power game en-
gineered with sleight-of-hand, with pandemic fear, and, where
black pawns like Trueblood are concerned, with undisguised
threats and intimidation. If Bledsoe is "a leader, a 'statesman'"
more than just the president of a college, he is also the "coal black
daddy" whose "magic" patriarchal leadership is a reign of terror
capable, he informs the narrator, of having "every Negro in the
country hanging on tree limbs" to sustain itself. Again, it is
through Trueblood, who is forced to checkmate Bledsoe's machinations against him with the equally treacherous power of the
white bosses, that Bledsoe is first unveiled as Norton's counterpart
and accomplice – a shape-shifting, mask-wearing "lyncher of
souls."

As Trueblood focuses Ellison's leadership calculus in the southern context, so the zoot-suited trio in New York's subway underground provides a focal image for unmasking the character of
leadership in the urban North. There, in symbolic tableau, Ellison's
meditations on Raglan's heroic mythology and the problem of
black leadership converge explicitly in a riddle of cultural creativity that his 1942 *Negro Quarterly* editorials had proposed as a functional test in political decipherment for those who would be masters of social movements.[6] Ellison's assertion then that the zoot
suit, or the symmetrical frenzy of the Lindy-hop, might conceal
"profound political meaning" crucial to black leaders expands
here, in the wake of the genuinely tragic death of Tod Clifton (the
novel's most idealized figure of political possibility), into a meta-
physical consolidation of all of those notions of history, culture,
consciousness, art, war, and dominion that the ritual progress of
the hero-narrator has cumulatively brought to the surface.

Looming suddenly before the narrator as silent, ambiguous figures with hard conked hair and bodies reshaped by costume into
the semblance of "African sculptures, distorted in the interest of a
design," the trio move before the narrator's finally unfettered vision "like dancers in some kind of funeral ceremony" (430). They
score their movements unself-consciously with the rhythmic
streetcorner staccato of tap dance, and share a puzzling and complete absorption in, significantly enough, comic books. The nar-

rator's jolting perception here is one of the book's true epiphanies. He realizes that, though "outside history" like Clifton after his plunge from Brotherhood, the zoot suiters might actually be "saviors, the true leaders" of an unfathomably irrational counterhistory. This revelation is succeeded by his seeing too that they are not anomalies but part of a whole uptown populace of "surreal variations" on downtown styles. The narrator now no longer sees that populace as a fixed mass to be led, but as a mysteriously fluid configuration of personalities and motives in terms of which his own capacities for leading must be recalculated and his ideal of leadership and its genesis reexamined. At this moment before his belief in Brotherhood has been completely blasted, that ideal is still represented by the talismanic image of Frederick Douglass. But "what was I in relation to the boys," he now must ask himself, and replies, "Perhaps an accident, like Douglass" – glimpsing here that the presumably "scientific" linkage between a leader and the led might, like the boys themselves, instead be outside science and the "groove of history" (432–3).

Douglass is the book's only undiminished historical image of knowledge and power humanely united. (Marcus Garvey, who is fleetingly praised by Clifton for his apparent ability to move a people who "are hell to move," is diminished implicitly by his association with Ras the Exhorter, just as Washington is diminished by explicit connection with the Founder, the Brotherhood, and the battle royal.) And Douglass is joined here in the narrator's mind with himself and Clifton, each of them gauged against the cryptic political possibilities of the comic-book-reading, zoot-suited boys. Until his experience of Rinehart and then Dupre and Scofield and their cadre of "rational" rioters completes this initial vision, the narrator will have no fuller revelation of leadership's inverse points of reference.

Rinehart, the "confidencing sonofabitch" who is a darker brother of Melville's Confidence Man, becomes Ellison's "personification of chaos." Rinehart pushes the calculus of leadership to its logical extreme and the narrator's political consciousness past thinking it *his* job somehow to get the zoot-suiters and their surreal brethren back inside the groove of history. In his grasp of the "vast seething, hot world of fluidity" beneath official history, and in his adjustment to modern life's fullest possibilities, Rinehart is the narrative's ultimate image of social mastery. A connoisseur of techniques and machines and a consummate decoder of the dark recesses of the human soul, he is, as he advertises, a "spiritual technologist" whose ability to manipulate private dreams, public myth, and symbolic structures like the zoot suit, the lindy-hop, storefront revivals, or sexual fantasy makes him potentially a more powerful leader than a man of principle such as Tod Clifton. Clifton is acknowledged even by his rival, Ras, as a natural leader, a "black prince." And Clifton, like Rinehart, understands the zoot-suiters better than the narrator ever will. But Clifton is fatally *misled* by his fervent belief in Brotherhood to *misread* the ulterior motives of his comrades. By contrast, Rinehart's "smooth tongue and heartless heart" and his willingness to do *anything* bespeak an utter lack of sentimentality about human vices and values and a cynicism that runs deeper and purer even than that of Ras. Ras "works on the inside" as effectively as Rinehart, and Ras is better able than Clifton or the narrator to penetrate the fog of Brotherhood ideology and to identify his natural enemies and allies. But his atavistic impulses distance him from the hypermodern world of the zoot-suiters and keep him from mastering the pragmatic techniques of empowerment.

If in the narrative's agrarian zone Bledsoe and Norton have proven themselves incapable of accommodating Trueblood's sensibility and its implications for genuine leadership, in the urban context Brother Jack, Ras, and Clifton as well, all prove inadequate to the task of leading zoot-suited Harlem. Only Rinehart is technically and metaphysically equipped to lead, but he is the most demonic mis-leader of all. Not surprisingly, the narrator's decision to take Rinehart as his model, and Rinehartism as his political instrument for undermining the Brotherhood's confidence, boomerangs – as have all of his preceding instrumentalities. First of all, he lacks the ruthlessness necessary to carry out the sexual intrigue he plans as a reversal of the Brotherhood's earlier efforts to neutralize him through the agency of a white woman. Then, after discovering a certain horrific sameness between the Brotherhood's real attitudes toward its Harlem constituents and Rinehart's – the Brotherhood's admitted "trick" of leadership is "to take advantage of them in their own best interest" – he finds that his counterapplication of Rinehart's cynical tactics leads not to the destruction of the Brotherhood, as he intends, but to the apocalyptic riots that the Brotherhood has helped engineer with his and Ras's unwitting complicity, making Harlem a dark sacrifice to political expediency.

The moment at which Jack-the-Bear commits himself to political Rinehartism, though, is another moment of epiphany, building on the perceptions that the trio in zoot suits had triggered. Here the reader witnesses the invisible man's first full acceptance of his personal past and its humiliations, his sense now of suddenly being able "to look around corners," his subsequent look around such a psychic corner to see Jack and Norton and Emerson "merge into one single white figure" of bat-blind absurdity. Here at last comes the narrator's first full recognition of his invisibility and his admission that, though he still didn't know what his grandfather's riddling strategy meant, he "was ready to test his advice." That the moment structures an even more comprehensive synthesis, one not yet fully known to the now very knowing narrator, is signaled in the punning metaphor he culls to link the contradictions of invisibility with the political exigencies of the moment: "I *was* and yet I was invisible . . . I was and yet I was unseen . . . Now I saw that I could agree with Jack without agreeing. And I could tell Harlem to have hope when there was no hope . . . *I would have to move them without myself being moved* . . . I'd have to do a Rinehart" (496).

The invisible man's role of inspiring emotion and action in others while remaining detached from the rhetoric of inspiration, the task of "having to move without being moved," is one that the narrator now links to Rinehart's confidencing maneuvers. It also is a provocative echo and revision of the precise terms in which Jim Trueblood had recounted his incestuous somnambulistic "tight spot" astride his daughter and alongside his wife. Trueblood comes to see the phallic dilemma he had awakened to as a metaphor for his life in general: Having "to move without moving" had *been* his predicament on the socioeconomic and political ladder, as it had then *become* his sole salvation from sexual sin. At authorial behest, Trueblood expresses here a psychological sense of context

175

akin to the seventh and most ambiguous of William Empson's seven types of ambiguity: that involving absolute opposites that define a center of conflict and that, like dreams in Freudian analysis, place in stereoscopic contradiction what one wants but has not got with what one has but cannot avoid, a conflict unresolvable save in another dimension beyond syntax and logic — in feeling rather than thought, in poetry rather than philosophy.

Short of some such resolving power in another dimension, the only material escape for Trueblood lay in the unmanning possibilities of a gelding knife, a mode of escape from context whose price, for as manly a "daddy quail" as Trueblood feels himself to be, is "too much to pay to keep from sinnin'" (59). In his full awareness, then, of the irredeemable cost of freedom from sin and the attendant consequences of freely sinning, Trueblood gives eloquent testimony to his own tragic sense of life and to that need for transcendence he finally satisfies only in the resolving poetry of the blues. Thus he is marked off in his own mind, as he later will be in the narrator's mind as well, from that world of mastery without limits, beyond ethics and love and art — beyond flesh-and-blood humanity — that the narrator discovers in the disembodied traces of Bliss Proteus Rinehart.[7] A matter of potent political import for the novel, Rinehart and Trueblood are ultimately the *non*political poles of sensibility between which the narrator must mediate his own ambiguous sense of freedom as necessity *and* as possibility. Despite Rinehart's unmediated freedom and Trueblood's subjection to psychic and social necessity, what Rinehart and Trueblood share is their existential awareness that to be free one must be able to "move without moving," a problem that Rinehart *masters* but Trueblood *transcends*.[8]

In this oblique contrast rests the staunchest fusing power of the narrator's Prologue and Epilogue to his tale, though Rinehart appears there only fleetingly and Trueblood not at all. Here, the narrator declares that both his underground hibernation and his prosecution of his grandfather's guerrilla war are at an end: Political action and love and responsibility are still possible, he decides. And he realizes that he wants neither Rinehart's freedom nor Jack's power. In so resolving, he recapitulates *consciously* Trueblood's ultimate rededication to his family, to seeing his "black 'bomination" birthed and not aborted, and to accepting his life's agonizing limits as perhaps inescapable but nevertheless endurable. If Trueblood's phallic dream has led him unconsciously to the brink of abysmal sexual sin and he has refused to unman himself to keep from sinning, so the narrator's political tactics – which finally implicate him in Clifton's death and the bloody Harlem riots – lead him unconsciously to the brink of a social abyss. And *his* phallic dream there of being unmanned girds his final refusal to substitute Rinehart's mode of moving without moving for Trueblood's.

In the Epilogue, Jack-the-Bear's will to so refuse is no desperate leap of faith denying the cumulative truth of his bruising, boomeranging experiences. Nor is it simply an expression of the bourgeois qualm that Rinehart's nihilism is criminally antisocial. Rather, the narrator's reborn will consolidates the patterned affirmations in his tale, which all along the way have counterpointed the chaotic reversals and explosions of negativity that otherwise dominate his movement through life. These affirmations constitute nothing so formidable as to subdue the forces of negation he has come to know: Though recurring throughout, they are momentary at best, isolated from the centers of pragmatic power, and often ambiguous in their own right. Most characteristically, they surface in the stream of resurgent folkloric figures and images from childhood that give his ritual experiences much of their emotional texture and hold him back from cultural deracination.

At their highest pitch, they form a rhythm of epiphany and gestaltic unification that forcefully defies the rule of chaos and destruction and dehumanization. The first and most resounding of these affirmations comes, again, in Jim Trueblood's cathartically sacred and profane riff, his church song–spawned blues. This creative will to transcendence asserts itself repeatedly in the narrative, often in reaction to, or anticipation of, the most dispiriting circumstances. The narrator, waiting for the hypocritically stage-managed "black rites of Horatio Alger" to begin in his college chapel, drifts into a countervailing reverie of himself, "the bungling bugler of words, imitating the trumpet and the trombone's timbre," that sweeps him away from Bledsoe's officious exercise in cynicism into a loving, lyrical paean to the silent, gray-haired campus matron, Miss Susie Gresham, an old "relic of slavery" who is beyond being "fooled with the mere content of words" and who bears "something warm and vital and all-enduring, of which in that island of shame we were not ashamed" (111–12). There also at vespers, counterpointing the sterility and meaninglessness of official ritual, he witnesses a sequence of *a capella* song and spontaneous prayer that simultaneously possesses the unnamed singer – her "voice seemed to become a disembodied force that sought to enter her, to violate her, shaking her rocking her rhythmically, as though it had become the source of her being." And witnessing her reduces the audience to "profound silence" (114–15).

Similarly, up North and alone, caught emotionally between his lingering country ways and his citified aspirations, the narrator encounters a loquacious yam vendor, yields to temptation and nostalgia, and then, on devouring the hot buttered yam, experiences an "intense feeling of freedom" and exhilaration. That feeling blossoms into a triumphantly comic fantasy confrontation with Bledsoe and prepares the narrator, unwittingly, for his succeeding eruption of indignation at a streetcorner eviction scene, which propels him into a new life as a professional rabble-rouser. Here as elsewhere in the narrative, the moment of affirmation is a moment also of self-unification – of mind, feelings, and physiology harmonized and expressively eloquent. The subsequent progress of his career as a Brotherhood orator is marked by a tension between his self-consciously controlled techniques or ideology and his spontaneous eruptions of compelling emotion. The ideological taboos that Jack imposes and the subject–object separation that Rinehart's smooth-tongued rhetoric requires are overruled in the moments of true union with his hearers and with his deepest understandings. He is most moving when moved himself.

At Tod Clifton's funeral, the invisible man's driving eulogy for his fallen brother is preceded by a moment of transcendent affirmation in which the funeral procession, ambiguously poised between love and "politicized hate," is transformed by the unprompted rise of a single plaintive, anonymous voice and the euphonium horn that rises to accompany it on "There's Many a Thousand Gone" (440ff). The funeral procession becomes, in spirit, a march. The young marchers join the old; the white marchers blend with the black. Singing "with his whole body, phrasing each verse as naturally as he walked," the first singer, an old man, becomes leader and follower simultaneously, un-self-consciously voicing "the old longing, resigned transcendent emotion" beneath the words. And by moving the crowd with "something deeper than protest, or religion," the anonymous elder unifies them into a powerful "singing mass" – and moves the narrator to wet-eyed wonder, and to envy also, as he confronts in the otherwise un-leaderly, knife-scarred old man the resplendent powers and art of leadership he has struggled so long to master.

In this dramatic image of art and leadership conjoined, the undergirding logic of the narrator's Epilogue optimism reveals itself. For the problems of heroic leadership in *Invisible Man* through which Ellison focused his extrapolations from myth, folk tradition, history, and political philosophy ultimately move toward resolution through an assimilation of the myth of the birth of the hero to the myth of the birth of the artist. Though rarely read in such terms, the novel is, as Ellison has quietly insisted, a "portrait of the *artist* as rabble-rouser" (*SA*, 179).

That the novel has few of the aesthetic signposts of conventional *Kunstlerroman* creates part of the confusion. Save for a brief punning allusion to the prototypic Joycean portrait of the artist, only in the framing Prologue and Epilogue is the theme of aesthetic idealism explicitly joined in the narrator's mind to his ritual struggle with politics and invisibility. And there it is not *his* oratorical art but the music of Louis Armstrong that functions as an index of cultivated sensibility and creative conflict. Ellison was clearly aware that narratives of artistic evolution frequently have a ritual substructure paralleling that of the mythic hero-king. The genealogy of talent admits the same dramatic dislocations and confusions as the genealogy of hereditary power. As a zone of adventure and contest, the world of artistic means and motives offers its own endemic monsters, mazes, and underworld terrain. And the patterns of quest and conquest inhere in the struggle for technique, style, and aesthetic vision no less than in the world that the heroes of myth inhabit. But in *Invisible Man* the psychological drama of the narrator's undesigned, un-self-conscious evolution as an artist is *veiled* by his conscious, designing passion for political heroism.

His explicit struggle to master the techniques of oratory, for example, registers only subliminally as an artist's labor to fashion a personal style. He focuses not on creating and expressing his own sensibility but on affecting and directing others. And the object of his artful pragmatism is not to communicate a vision of beauty or unalloyed truth as a subject for contemplation, but to spur the acquisition of practical power by moving men and women to action.

In such a context, he becomes conscious of himself as an artist only when his failure as a hero seems complete. In the Prologue and Epilogue, as ranter turned writer, he has supplanted his original quest for Washingtonian leadership with a quest for yet to be discovered forms of overt action intimated musically in the heroic lyricism of Louis Armstrong's blues. If here it seems uncertain that he has anything more than revived illusion to sustain a hinted future return to rabble-rousing or to "playing a role" – if Armstrong might be only an ambiguous new mirage to "keep this nigger boy running" – nevertheless Ellison's theory and concept-toting "thinker-tinker" does repudiate his former illusions. And he does draw a cautionary veil of consciousness between Armstrong and himself: Louis has made "poetry out of invisibility" because he is *unaware* that he is invisible. The inference is that being unaware may give Armstrong a creative edge, at least provisionally. For awareness, Jack-the-Bear has learned, in its initial stages, insofar as it illuminates the awesome forces of chaos and unfreedom without vouchsafing countervailing strategies, need be no boon at all; it may rather be a burden, a burden from which Armstrong apparently is free. Jack-the-Bear's own compulsion to "put invisibility down in black and white," he ruminates, may be an analogous urge to make *music* of invisibility – to annex the musician's powers of synesthetic perception to the more limited ones available to a man who has chosen to be "an orator, a rabble-rouser . . . and perhaps shall be again" (14).

Jack-the-Bear has been a man of words; but because words cannot contain all of reality, his dependence on them prescribes failures and confusions from which the maker of music is comparatively freer. The Word's entanglement with scientific and historical rationality and denotative constraints bars the penetration into time and space that music's relative elusiveness and freedom from official intelligibility make possible. And his memoir's riddling problem of freedom is, he discovers, unresolvable apart from a decipherment of the culture's and his own consciousness of time. He enunciates time's strategic possibilities in his recollection of a prizefighter boxing a yokel and his seeing the former's vastly superior science, speed, and footwork knocked "cold as a well digger's posterior" when the yokel simply steps inside his opponent's sense of time to deliver a single felling blow. What the narrator discovers vaguely in the "nodes" and "breaks" of Armstrong's music is such a sense of time.

Music – bound more than any of the other arts to time and timing – was for Ellison, even more than for his music-minded novelistic exemplar, Malraux, that expressive penetration into ultimate reality whose forms, patterns of evolution, traditions, and metamorphoses supplied the clues not only to the souls of black folk but to the rhythms and style and soul of modern civilization. For such inquisitors of modern life as Hegel, Nietzsche, Spengler, and Yeats, the cycles and spirals and gyres hypothetically circumscribing the course of human events were mimed and ofttimes mocked by the shifting forms of art, literature, *and especially music.* For these thinkers, the old romanticist ethos and its expressive theory of art were raised to cosmic significance. In Malraux's view, it was the drama of art confronting the world and refusing to follow the "natural" order that the visual arts especially, and music more than literature, recorded in their own autonomous history.[9] And that history, a history of "style" and the mysterious logic through which style unfolds and imposes itself on the world, is the history whose structured principles in blues and jazz and vernacular signification and folk fable Ellison's narrator ultimately wields against the structure of lies and illusions that have dominated and diminished the sense of possibility he had discovered as an invisible man:

> My God, what possibilities existed! And that spiral business, that progress goo. . . . And that lie that success was a rising *upward.* What a crummy lie they kept us dominated by. Not only could you travel upward toward success but you could travel downward as well; up *and* down, in retreat as well as in advance, crabways and

crossways and around in a circle, meeting your old selves coming
and going and perhaps all at the same time. (498–9)

Such multidimensional possibilities are visible to the musician
more than the man of words because, as the irresistible "club" of
reality has impressed on Jack-the-Bear, there is "an area in which
a man's feelings are more rational than his mind." And music,
freed from the constraints of ordinary linguistic thought, maps it
more completely than communicative rhetoric, which, however
much it strives to expand its symbolic powers, replicates only a
fragment of the vast repertoire of human expressive possibilities
manifest in grins, growls, and gestures on to the masterpieces of
high art and the wizardry of machines. The liberating possibilities
of music, however, remain untapped because music, he admits, is
perceived one-dimensionally – "is heard and seldom *seen* except
by musicians" (13). Conversely, as his hallucinogenic hyperper-
ceptivity teaches him, when music's full synesthetic possibilities
are grasped by the perceiver, its explorations into time and space
may be so overwhelming as to actually "inhibit action" and defy
the political will expressed in the narrator's own undaunted belief
"in *nothing* if not in action" (13).

If the "laws" of history impose a tyranny of time, circumstance,
and conceptual limitation on humanity, Armstrong's art, Trueblood's, the singer of spirituals, and the psychic geometries of the
zoot suit offer escape from the bondage of history, not through any
evasion of circumstance but through the evocation and consolidation of styles and attitudes for confronting it. In Malraux's psychology of art, which Ellison converted enthusiastically to his own
ends in the late forties, this "deflection" of history is rooted in a
resurrection of the conventional romantic elevation of creative
genius and of the artist as hero: Living in time, but also in the
presence of the timeless world where art's collective testimony
prevails regardless of the change and mortality outside, the artist
"escapes" ordinary history – and historical fatalism – in those
isolated moments of unique creativity when the expressive gesture
liberates him or her from inherited traditions and reveals a style
entirely his or her own.[10] In making such creative gestures, the
artist participates in a "history" of creative events, in moments of

creative heroism that constitute their own continuity, deflected from, if sometimes parallel to, conventional history.

For Ellison, the danger of trying to escape into this antihistory by way of either the creative or the religious imagination was manifest in the Afro-American past, where, as he decried in his 1945 review of Wright's *Black Boy*, the special conditions of black life and its consequently "defensive character" had regularly transformed the "will toward organization" into a "will to camouflage, to dissimulate" (*SA*, 93). Creative heroism, for Malraux and Wright and Ellison, could be energized only by a will to confront both the world of circumstance and the world of creative gesture. Creative power manifested itself in the capacity to *transcend* circumstance – by experiencing it directly, exploring it exhaustively, and then reintegrating it by acts of willed imagination in such a way as to remake potentially the culture of which it is a part. The attraction of the blues, their manifest power, lay in their discovery of a *style* for expressing simultaneously the agony of life and the possibility of conquering it. Rather than a flight into aestheticism or a passive cultivation of sensibility, they were a codified assertion of will – if not overtly political, then nonetheless allied with the political will to convert, through action, conscious experience into felt power.

To unify the political will and the creative will against the backdrop of sweeping historical change and of human values confronting such change was Ralph Ellison's most ambitious intention as a novelist. That his tragicomic judgment of the characters he places under such pressure veers finally toward aesthetic norms and away from the narrowly political links him, of course, to such acknowledged literary "ancestors" and "relatives" as Malraux, again, and to Hemingway, Miguel de Unamuno, and, more obliquely, Richard Wright. For the former three, the interpenetration into extreme human situations of such aesthetic norms as grace, balance, contemplative detachment, and élan was central to the drama of the heroic. In *Invisible Man*, Louis Armstrong's projective sense of style – which culminates the novel's long series of creative gestures and affirmations in extremity – is Ellison's clearest corollary: It is Armstrong who personifies the narrator's consummatory maxim that "humanity is won by continuing to play in the face of certain defeat" (564); and it is Armstrong who, as he "bends" his military instrument into a beam of lyrical sound, carries Jim Trueblood's country blues standard, by phonograph, into the narrative's urban fray.

But Ellison's invisible man knows that for all of Trueblood's and Armstrong's flesh-and-bone wisdom and their lyric aplomb, the bluesmen have styled *preliminary* attitudes and *transcendental* resolutions of conflicts whose possible solution through material means he, not they, is better suited by proximity to power, by technique, *and by consciousness* to undertake. That Trueblood and Armstrong are unaware of their invisibility – as the narrator's grandfather also had been – is both their advantage and their limitation. Unlike Rinehart, whose freedom is a destructive freedom that feeds on illusion and breeds chaos and death, and whose victory over the material world is won at the cost of absolute self-effacement, Armstrong does not trade on invisibility and is not self-diminished by it. He has transcended defeat by imposing his own personality on his horn and converting its "Bad Air" to communal poetry. In so doing, he has asserted his own undefeated will and defies death itself with an indestructible artistry. Without the strategically crucial sense of space and time that conscious invisibility provides, however, extending his conquest of the world of art into the world of material circumstances remains a hope limited by the ability of his auditors to hear truly.

In Malraux's world, the problem of art's pragmatic relation to the pattern of material existence remains characteristically unresolved. The hero-revolutionaries of his political novels and the artist-heroes of his aesthetic essays are spiritually related but kept consistently apart. The humorless political heroes, inevitably defeated by the failure or betrayal of social revolution, choose consciously to act out doomed commitments they can no longer see as anything but absurd and to martyr themselves, as in *Man's Fate*, to their transcendent passion for the ideal. The hero-artists, by contrast, escape the world of men, in which freedom is finally impossible, steal creative fire from the gods, and in their own self-constructed world of art win the freedom that the hero-revolutionaries can only imagine. Ellison's impulse in *Invisible Man* was to

184

reject forms of transcendence limited either to final political martyrdom or to a hermetic world of aesthetics, and instead to unify the dissevered possibilities in the figure of a political man of words and action redeemed and reborn through art. If Richard Wright, like Malraux and Hemingway, cleaved to a secular vision of heroic, or antiheroic, martyrdom in *Native Son,* Ellison in *Invisible Man* found it possible, indeed necessary, both to reject the cult of death and to affirm the hope of spiritual rebirth by recording symbolically his group's *true* pan-generational transcendence of material defeat through the agencies of art.

As his own immersion in his people's and his nation's history had taught him, and as he would later remark, "the art – the blues, the spiritual, the jazz, the dance – was what we had in place of freedom" (*SA*, 254–5). Rather than proposing any substitutional or merely compensatory role for art, *Invisible Man* makes artistic transcendence the one unsuppressible means through which human freedom is imagined and achieved and human beings made whole. Its narrator's torturing himself to put down in black and white the chronicle of his abysmal pain, and the progress through illusion to perception that enables him to see the pattern in its chaos, carry to a higher level that articulate probing of a grievous wound that Jim Trueblood modeled for him with tale and defeat-defying blues. The telling of his own tale – his "buggy jiving" – is the hibernating narrator's initial reengagement with a world that still conspires to defeat him. It is a cathartic release of anger and angst that, through the power of words, converts what begins as an act of war into what he finally knows has become an act of disarmament. And it is, on the terms its author proposes, an act of conscious leadership in which one man's will to selfhood brings to comic and tragic clarity his and his reader-followers' common property in the buggy, jiving, blue-black rites of man.

NOTES

1. Ralph Ellison, "On Initiation Rites and Power: Ralph Ellison Speaks at West Point," ed. Robert H. Moore, *Contemporary Literature,* 15 (1974);170–1.

2. Ralph Ellison, *Shadow and Act* (New York: Random House, 1964), p. 177. This volume will be cited hereafter as *SA*.
3. Frederick Karl, *The Adversary Literature: The English Novel in the Eighteenth Century* (republished as *A Reader's Guide to the Eighteenth Century English Novel*) (New York: Farrar, Straus and Giroux, 1974), pp. 14–18.
4. Ibid., p. 17.
5. See Harry Levin, *The Power of Blackness: Hawthorne, Poe, Melville* (New York: Knopf, 1958).
6. Ralph Ellison, "Editorial Comment," *The Negro Quarterly*, 1 (Winter–Spring 1943):295–302.
7. Ellison states the character's full name in *Shadow and Act*, p. 56.
8. For an aptly focused explication of this recurring motif in its initial setting in *Invisible Man*, see Houston Baker, "To Move without Moving: An Analysis of Creativity and Commerce in Ralph Ellison's Trueblood Episode," *PMLA*, 98 (October 1983):828–45.
9. William Righter, *The Rhetorical Hero: An Essay on the Aesthetics of André Malraux* (London: Routledge & Kegan Paul, 1964), pp. 21–5.
10. Ibid., p. 41; and Avriel Goldberger, *Visions of a New Hero: The Heroic Life According to André Malraux and Earlier Advocates of Human Grandeur* (Paris: M. J. Minard, 1965), pp. 234–43.

Notes on Contributors

John Callahan teaches English at Lewis and Clark College in Portland, Oregon. He is the author of *The Illusions of a Nation: Myth and History in the Novels of F. Scott Fitzgerald* and *In the African-American Grain: The Pursuit of Voice in Twentieth Century Black Fiction.*

Robert O'Meally, Professor of English and Afro-American Studies at Wesleyan University, is the author of *The Craft of Ralph Ellison.*

Berndt Ostendorf is director of the Amerika-Institut at the University of Munich, where he holds the chair in American cultural history. He is the author of *Mythos in der Neuen Welt, Black Literature in White America,* and *Gettoliteratur.*

Thomas Schaub is Associate Professor of English at the University of Wisconsin, Madison. He is the author of *Pynchon: The Voice of Ambiguity.*

Valerie Smith is Associate Professor of English at Princeton University. She has published several articles on recent Afro-American literature; her book *Self-Discovery and Authority in Afro-American Narrative* is forthcoming from Harvard University Press.

John Wright is Chairman of Afro-American and African Studies at the University of Minnesota. His manuscript *The Riddle of Freedom: Art, Ideas, and the Contours of Afro-American Literary Thought* is being prepared for publication.

Selected Bibliography

The edition of *Invisible Man* that is cited by all of the contributors to this volume is the paperback Thirtieth Anniversary Edition, issued by Vintage Books of Random House in 1982. That edition is complete, correct, and readily available; and it includes an indispensable introductory essay by the author. It is also recommended that readers look at the Franklin Mint Edition of 1980 for the sake of its more compressed author's preface. The illustrations in this edition, however, recall those in the special edition of Ernest Hemingway's *A Farewell to Arms* and Hemingway's reactions to them, as recorded in his Preface: "Unless the artist is as good or better a painter or draftsman than the writer is a writer, there can be no more disappointing thing than for the writer to see the things and the places and the people that he remembers making drawn and put on paper by some one else who was not there."

It remains to be noted that in the Thirtieth Anniversary Edition, the following dates appear on the publication page: 1947, 1948, 1952, and February 1972; this edition itself appeared in 1982. The novel's actual date of first publication is 1952, hence that date. Its first chapter appeared in an English magazine, *Horizon,* in 1947, and then in an American magazine, *'48 Magazine of the Year,* in 1948. February 1972 refers to the first issue of the Vintage paperback edition.

Anderson, Jervis. "Going to the Territory." *New Yorker,* 52 (November 22, 1976):55–108.

Baker, Houston A. Jr., *Blues, Ideology, and Afro-American Literature.* Chicago: University of Chicago Press, 1984.

Benston, Kimberly W., "Ellison, Baraka, and the Faces of Tradition." *boundary 2,* 6 (Winter 1978):333–54.

Callahan, John F. "The Historical Frequencies of Ralph Waldo Ellison." In *Chant of Saints,* ed. Michael S. Harper and Robert B. Stepto. Urbana: University of Illinois Press, 1979, pp. 33–52.

The Carleton Miscellany, 18 (Winter 1980); special Ellison issue.

College Language Association. *CLA Journal,* 13 (March 1970); special Ellison issue.

Covo, Jacqueline. *The Blinking Eye: Ralph Waldo Ellison and His American, French, German and Italian Critics, 1952–1971.* Metuchen, N.J.: Scarecrow Press, 1974.

Delta, 18 (April 1984); special Ellison issue, published in Paris.

Dietze, Rudolf F. *Ralph Ellison: The Genesis of an Artist.* Nuremberg: Hans Carl, 1982.

Hersey, John, ed. *Ralph Ellison, a Collection of Critical Essays.* Englewood Cliffs, N.J.: Prentice-Hall, 1974.

Howe, Irving. *A World More Attractive.* New York: Horizon Press, 1963.

Hyman, Stanley Edgar. *The Promised End.* New York: World Publishing, 1963.

List, Robert N. *Dedalus in Harlem.* Washington, D.C.: University Press of America, 1982.

Murray, Albert. *The Omni-Americans.* New York: Outerbridge and Diensfrey, 1970.

O'Meally, Robert G. *The Craft of Ralph Ellison.* Cambridge, Mass.: Harvard University Press, 1980.

Reilly, John M., ed. *Twentieth Century Interpretations of Invisible Man: A Collection of Essays.* Englewood Cliffs, N.J.: Prentice-Hall, 1970.

Stepto, Robert B. *From Behind the Veil: A Study of Afro-American Narrative.* Urbana: University of Illinois Press, 1979.

Trimmer, Joseph F. *A Casebook on Ralph Ellison's Invisible Man.* New York: Thomas Y. Crowell, 1972.